Dates for the exhibition:

THE BALTIMORE MUSEUM OF ART
1 May-10 June 1973

THE COLUMBUS GALLERY OF FINE ARTS, Ohio
12 July-26 August 1973

WORCESTER ART MUSEUM, Massachusetts
19 September-28 October 1973

JOSLYN ART MUSEUM, Omaha, Nebraska
19 November-23 December 1973

MUNSON-WILLIAMS-PROCTOR INSTITUTE, Utica,
  New York
20 January-24 February 1974

THEODORE ROBINSON, 1852-1896

Introduction and Commentary by Sona Johnston

THE BALTIMORE MUSEUM OF ART

THEODORE ROBINSON, 1852-1896

Introduction and Commentary by Sona Johnston

THE BALTIMORE MUSEUM OF ART

List of Lenders

ADDISON GALLERY OF AMERICAN ART, Phillips Academy, Andover, Massachusetts, *42*
ART INSTITUTE OF CHICAGO, *22*
THE ART MUSEUM, Princeton University, New Jersey, *38*
BABCOCK GALLERIES, New York, *58*
THE BROOKLYN MUSEUM, New York, *21, 29, 37*
CANAJOHARIE LIBRARY AND ART GALLERY, Canajoharie, New York, *30*
CHAPELLIER GALLERIES, New York, *25*
CINCINNATI ART MUSEUM, Ohio, *47*
COLBY COLLEGE ART MUSEUM, Waterville, Maine, *14*
THE COLUMBUS GALLERY OF FINE ARTS, Ohio, *57*
CLARIBEL CONE, II, Scarsdale, New York, *51*
CORCORAN GALLERY OF ART, Washington, D. C., *43, 48*
MR. AND MRS. MAURICE GLICKMAN, New York, *8, 32*
MR. AND MRS. RAYMOND J. HOROWITZ, New York, *9, 27, 45*
KENNEDY GALLERIES, INC., New York, *4*
MR. AND MRS. PAUL LANDAU, New York, *1, 3*
FLORENCE LEWISON GALLERY, New York, *10*
MANN GALLERIES, Miami, Florida, *7*
THE METROPOLITAN MUSEUM OF ART, New York, *23, 46*
MONTCLAIR ART MUSEUM, New Jersey, *36*
MUSEUM OF ART, RHODE ISLAND SCHOOL OF DESIGN, Providence, *35*
MUSEUM OF FINE ARTS, St. Petersburg, Florida, *31*
NATIONAL ACADEMY OF DESIGN, New York, *17*
NATIONAL COLLECTION OF FINE ARTS, SMITHSONIAN INSTITUTION, Washington, D. C., *15*
NEBRASKA ART ASSOCIATION, Lincoln, *50*
NEW BRITAIN MUSEUM OF AMERICAN ART, New Britain, Connecticut, *56*
PENNSYLVANIA ACADEMY OF THE FINE ARTS, Philadelphia, *16, 49*
THE PHILLIPS COLLECTION, Washington, D. C., *24, 33*
PIEDMONT DRIVING CLUB, Atlanta, Georgia, *53*
MR. AND MRS. SAMUEL PORTER, Great Neck, New York, *52*
MR. AND MRS. MEYER POTAMKIN, *55*

iv

RANDOLPH-MACON WOMAN'S COLLEGE, Lynchburg, Virginia, *44*
MRS. JOHN BARRY RYAN, New York, *41*
SCRIPPS COLLEGE, Claremont, California, *40*
SMITH COLLEGE MUSEUM OF ART, Northampton, Massachusetts, *6*
IRA SPANIERMAN, INC., New York, *64, 65, 66*
STEVEN STRAW COMPANY, Seabrook, New Hampshire, *13*
UNIVERSITY OF KANSAS MUSEUM, Lawrence, *5*
MR. AND MRS. WILLIAM YOUNG, Wellesley Hills, Massachusetts, *28*
ANONYMOUS *2, 11, 26, 34, 54, 59, 60, 61, 62, 63*
FROM THE COLLECTION OF THE BALTIMORE MUSEUM OF ART, *12, 18, 19, 20, 39*

Foreword

This is the first major museum exhibition of Theodore Robinson's painting since 1946, and The Baltimore Museum of Art is pleased to have this role in providing an opportunity for re-appraising his work. Renewed interest in American painting during the last few years makes this an especially appropriate time for a comprehensive exhibition of Robinson's work. In addition, Robinson's paintings have a very special place in the collections of the Baltimore Museum.

Even before her first trip to Europe in 1901, Etta Cone had begun the journey into the world of art which was to lead her and her sister Claribel into assembling the remarkable Cone Collection, now housed in The Baltimore Museum of Art. The cornerstone of that Collection is a group of paintings by Theodore Robinson, four of which remain in the Collection today. They were acquired at the sale of Robinson's estate in 1898, and as her sister Bertha wrote to Etta Cone in March 1898, "I hope you will be delighted with them and that they will greatly help make your parlor the delightful room you want." This kind of very personal relationship to the purchase of works of art guided the Cone sisters as they developed their Collection. The straightforward view of the world with an emphasis on color and light, so characteristic of Theodore Robinson's paintings, foretells the aesthetic sensibilities of Etta and Dr. Claribel Cone which are so evident in the later, better-known acquisitions.

I am grateful to Sona Johnston, Assistant Curator of Painting and Sculpture, for directing the exhibition and writing the perceptive essays and notes which accompany the catalogue. Ann Boyce Harper, Managing Editor, edited the publication, Margaret Powell read the manuscript, and Linda Bradley Norris typed the copy. Finally, on behalf of all the museums which are presenting this fresh view of Theodore Robinson's work, I thank the various lenders who have generously permitted such extended loans so that Robinson's paintings may become better known in this country.

Tom L. Freudenheim
Director

Introduction

There are two dominant factors in Theodore Robinson's life which had an immediate effect on his art. The first was the chronic illness to which he constantly had to make concessions throughout his short life; the second was his meeting in 1888 with Claude Monet. His frail health, although a negative element, was not only undoubtedly instrumental, from childhood on, in molding his somewhat retiring personality but also defined the boundaries to which he could extend his energies. His relationship with Monet, on the other hand, served to synthesize tendencies already apparent in his art in the mid-1880's into a personal impressionist style.

The artist Birge Harrison in his description of life among the group of men who summered at Grez in 1877, recalled Robinson during his student days as "a semi-invalid, a great sufferer from asthma, which never gave him a moment's respite. . . ." [1] Robinson's Diary which covers the years from 1892 to his death in 1896 contains many references, not specifically to his illness, but to the discomfort and depression of spirit which it produced. A Diary entry for 12 July 1892, written during his last summer at Giverny when he was at work on the *Valley of the Seine* series (cat. nos. 42-44), clearly reveals the extent of his struggle and its subsequent effect on his painting:

Am afraid I am losing time on my vues. They are perhaps too large for me—or I get
tired carrying my stuff so far—at any rate, they drag terribly. . . .

Such an entry has its antithesis as suggested in this enthusiastic notation made on 19 June 1894 at Cos Cob:

A smart shower at 2 p.m. The first for two weeks. Am getting well and strong and
work with interest—especially from the R.R. Bridge—late afternoon. the club-house
and little yachts at anchor, low-tide, patches of sea grass. It is particularly brilliant
at about 5 p.m.

1. Harrison, p. 307

Although of a speculative nature, one can draw certain conclusions as to the tangible effects of Robinson's ill health on his oeuvre. In general, his canvases tend to be small, easily manipulated in the out-of-doors. Frequently, this limitation in size is incongruous with the nature of the image he chose to depict. This is most evident in such expansive landscape views as the various representations of the Seine Valley or in the Napanoch or Cos Cob canvases done upon his return to America. His largest paintings, such as *The Layette* (cat. no. 48) or *La Vachère* (cat. no. 20) are figurative—a type of subject matter which probably necessitated less moving from spot to spot.

In many of Robinson's canvases, there is the feeling that certain elements are left unresolved. Many of them are successful beginnings, verging on completion, but somehow lack the unity and assurance of an idea carried through to its conclusions. Although probably not directly related to his frail constitution, this factor is more than likely the result of a state of mind which dominated him at certain adverse times. Robinson himself was aware of this shortcoming in his work, and he noted in his Diary in New York on 12 April 1894:

. . . my painting stops too soon, and I am too satisfied with the appearance (surface) without going on and giving that "special effort" of attention necessary not only for line, but for other qualities as well, refined color and modeling, discrimination between important and unimportant detail, etc.

Such personal critical observations are frequent, and one feels the tragedy of a man recognizing his ideals, yet being unable to meet them. In his article on Camille Corot written for John van Dyke's volume *Modern French Masters by American Artists*, published in 1896 shortly after his death, Robinson reveals what he so desperately had wanted for himself:

Truly an enviable existence was that of Corot. With a fine physique and a joyous temperament that enabled him to accept without bitterness the little recognition that was his for years, his success yet came in time for him to enjoy it. [2]

Robinson's stylistic development prior to his association with Claude Monet is worthy of some discussion. As with other Americans of his generation, his artistic training had been obtained at the academies first in New York and subsequently in Paris with Carolus-Duran, Gérôme, and Benjamin Constant. Their emphasis on draughtsmanship and on the careful rendering of form and volume is evident in the few canvases extant which date from the late 1870's and early 1880's (see cat. nos. 1-2) as well as from his sketchbooks of the period (cat. nos. 64-65).

2. Robinson, "Corot," p. 115

RIVER LANDSCAPE

(Cat. no. 11)

x

LA VACHÈRE (GIRL AND COW) 1888

(Cat. no. 20)

After his return to America at the conclusion of his formal studies, this sound academic training was combined with what he absorbed from the romantic subject matter used by the muralists, LaFarge and Treadwell, and the result in his paintings was a monumental figurative style. In essence, he scaled down the architectural decorations to easel size. The figures are strongly drawn, solid, and at times sculptural. Imbued with a sense of detachment from the viewer, either through a turned head or a trance-like gaze, they are rootless in time or place, their simple clothing merely suggesting some by-gone era. Although essentially confined to the mid-1880's (see cat. nos. 7-8) elements of this style can still be seen in his *Layette* of 1892 (cat. no. 48).

Another important aspect of Robinson's art which appears to have had its inception in the 1880's is his use of photography. There is evidence that he, like many of his fellow artists, used photographic studies from the early 1880's on, at which time he wrote the following to his family:

Painting directly from nature is difficult, as things do not remain the same, the camera helps to retain the picture in your mind.[3]

Robinson's photographs are full of contrasts of light and dark areas with very little suggestion of middle tones. Some details tend to be blurred, while others are lost in the patches of dark and light. Judging by those which still survive, Robinson, with very few exceptions, confined the use of the photographic study to his figurative works which may have an economic consideration since he did not feel he could spend the money for a model. His degree of dependency varies. In some instances, he appears to have closely copied the original ; other paintings reveal slight variations, primarily for considerations of composition (see cat. no. 33). Diary entries seem to reveal something of his method. One notation made at Giverny on 27 July 1892 indicates that he is at work on a painting "from a photo of Marie," but in another he is working from a live model in the setting.

In his landscape paintings, he used photographs in a slightly different manner. On 6 November of the same year, he writes that he "began a thing at 3:30 looking at little mill from the plain—things all around (skies) most lovely." On 28 November, a few days before his departure from Giverny, he records that he "took a photo of 'little mill' and commenced packing." More than likely the photograph would serve to recall the site as he completed the painting in his studio in New York.

Ultimately, Robinson was bothered by feelings of guilt at his dependency on the camera:

---

3. Baur, Brooklyn Museum, p. 36

WILLOWS (EN PICARDIE) ca. 1891

(Cat. no. 37)

*I don't know just why I do this . . . partly I fear because I am in N.Y. where other
men are doing this,—it is in the air.* (Diary, 31 January 1893) [4]

Indeed, numerous other artists were, including Winslow Homer for whom he had a lifelong
admiration.

Impressionism did not visibly influence Robinson's work until the mid-1880's but
his initial contact undoubtedly was in his first Parisian sojourn in 1876-79. The year of
his arrival in the French capital was marked by the second Impressionist exhibition held
at the galleries of Durand-Ruel on the rue le Peletier, and during his stay in France, two
others were held: one in 1877 and another in 1879. The 1870's were indeed great years for
Impressionism, and, however entrenched Robinson was in his academic studies, he must
certainly have seen the exhibitions and noted the storm of controversy which each in
turn provoked.

Robinson's contacts with Impressionism would have been reinforced in the 1880's when
the impact of the French movement began to be felt in America. J. Alden Weir, in Paris in
1881 to buy paintings for the New York collector Erwin Davis, had purchased through the
urging of William M.Chase, an early supporter of the Impressionists, Edouard Manet's
Boy with the Sword,[5] hardly a luminist painting but most assuredly a departure from the
previously-favored works of such artists as Bouguereau and Lefebvre.

The first real opportunity for the country to become acquainted with Impressionism
was in 1883 when a "Foreign Exhibition" opened in Boston at the Mechanics Building on
3 September. Included were works by Manet, Monet, Pissarro, Renoir and Sisley.[6] Again, it
is likely that Robinson may have seen the exhibition, as he was back and forth between
Boston and New York during the years 1882-84, engaged on various decorative murals.

As John Baur quite rightly points out in his 1946 monograph, Robinson's paintings of
the early 1880's which are not related to his decorative style (for example, Baur, nos. 97
& 151) are a logical outgrowth of the European experience merged with his native, realist
tendencies.[7] They are firmly-drawn, solid canvases, in the tradition of American genre
painting, yet they show more concern for color, tone and the qualities of light.

It is generally acknowledged that Robinson's Impressionist paintings date from the
beginning of his personal association with Claude Monet in 1888, yet it is evident from
what can be assumed was his previous knowledge and subsequent understanding of the
elements of the movement that he had adopted Impressionism in essence as early as 1886.
This is most readily apparent in his painting entitled *Girl With a Goat* (cat no. 13) which

4. Ibid., p. 36   5. Huth, p. 229   6. Ibid., p. 229   7. Baur, Brooklyn Museum, pp. 20-21

is signed and dated 1886. Local color almost disappears, and the flickering tones of reflected light on the surface of the various forms mark it as a transitional work.

Robinson, then, undoubtedly familiar with Claude Monet's work, settled in Giverny in 1888, already committed to the new approach and perhaps desiring to paint in the same locale as the man who was for him the personification of the movement. His devotion to Monet is clearly evident in a short article which he wrote that appeared in the September 1892 issue of *Century Magazine*, although it may have been written a year or so earlier. Essentially a defense rather than an interpretation or explanation, the emphasis of the article is on Monet's faithfulness to his image of nature:

To my mind, no one has yet painted out of doors quite so truly. He is a realist, believing that nature and our own day give us abundant and beautiful material for pictures: that, rightly seen and rendered, there is as much charm in a nineteenth-century girl in her tennis or yachting suit, and in a landscape of sunlit meadows or river-bank, as in the Lefebvre nymph with her appropriate but rather dreary setting of "classical landscape;" that there is an abundance of poetry outside of swamps, twilights or weeping damosels. [8]

Thus, Robinson saw Monet's art conceptually rather than technically, emphasizing the element of realism which was the all-important factor in his own art. Both viewed nature differently, yet each stressed a faithfulness to their vision. For Monet, the color is often vivid, the light brilliant, dissolving form and outline in a shimmering atmosphere. Monet had once advised an aspiring painter

try to forget what objects you have before you, a tree, a house, a field, or whatever. Merely think, here is a little square of blue, here an oblong of pink, here a streak of yellow, and paint it just as it looks to you. The exact color and shape, until it gives your own naive impression of the scene before you. [9]

In contrast, Robinson's colors are muted, the range of tone is deliberately limited, and there is a delight in closely-related harmonies. He did not abstract the image before him as Monet had advised. With few exceptions his forms remain solid, firmly-defined, and the subject matter is always clearly identifiable. Although the degree of his initial devotion to Monet's Impressionism is obvious, his art demonstrates a selection and subsequent interpretation of those elements most sympathetic to his manner of expression. And in the period between the writing of the *Century* article and its publication, Robinson's

8. Robinson, "Monet," p. 171   9. Seitz, p. 28

THE E.M.J. BETTY 1894

(Cat. no. 54)

zealousness had lessened. He had realized that his own goals differed from Monet's:

I like the spirit of the article—enthusiastic and written <u>con amore</u>—as I felt then
—the enthusiasm of the young convert. Now, I am unchanged—but perhaps less
exuberant in my liking. (Diary, Giverny, 8 September 1892).

Robinson returned to America, determined to expand his vision beyond the rural French countryside to the scenes of his homeland. Giverny had been the ideal setting for a "convert" to Impressionism, but ultimately it must have proved to be limiting to the artist who had evolved his own personal impressionistic style. If, indeed, Giverny had been a safe haven, it now offered no challenge and it is likely that Robinson, determined to remain faithful to his realism, sought a broader nature on which to draw.

Robinson's paintings of his American period from 1892 to his death in 1896 are primarily landscapes which testify to his adherence to the image before him. He seemed especially intent on guarding against any artificial or contrived element in his art. Shortly after his return to New York, he expressed this thought in his Diary:

. . . I believe it will be all the better for a painter to get back to the people's liking
of "views" and things in nature he had liked before he began to study and was told
what was the correct thing to admire—"bits," ruins . . . marshes, etc.
(20 February 1893).

And after a summer of teaching and painting at Napanoch he reiterated this feeling, stressing the beauty of the ordinary:

I'm sorry I've done nothing with the little square, box-shaped white houses, often
very pretty as notes and even more. Much can be done, I'm sure, by tackling anything
and everything, and not avoiding things very typical like our frame buildings. We
have been too much afraid of certain things, and I have been choosing things we
have painted abroad or similar ones—instead of painting as the Dutchmen did,
patiently and sincerely, their own kind of house, ugly as it may appear to some.
And new beauties, new oddities, new points of interest are awaiting discovery.
And it is surprising how well it looks, once on canvas. One or two of my canal
things are in a good direction, it seems to me, and still more courage, emancipation
from old formulae and ideas of what is interesting or beautiful, from the
European standpoint, will work wonders. (29 October 1893)

Several of the canal views (see cat. nos. 51-53) are indeed renderings of commonplace subjects, and in their fresh, straightforward representation of the image, they are clearly American.

Perhaps Robinson's most successful American canvases are those which he painted at Cos Cob during the summer of 1894 (see cat. nos. 54-55). Combined with the realism, there is a poetic quality, giving them that "special effort of attention" which he felt his paintings had lacked. It was in Townshend, Vermont, however, that Robinson claimed to have found his ideal setting. For the first time, he felt that he was painting subjects meaningful to him rather than merely "good bits." The canvases of the summer were disappointing and unresolved, and his Diary records the continual frustrations of attempting to reconcile the qualities of the landscape with his impressionistic method of painting. Perhaps the site itself was too reminiscent of the familiar Seine Valley, and he recognized in the Vermont canvases similarities to previous French works:

In a way, I believe I have lost time this summer, by trying to paint a particular effect and not taking what nature gave me; losing many excellent hours because I wanted something else, and perhaps I wanted to repeat a success viz: my "Valley of the Seine." I must think of this. (14 November 1895)

What another summer at Townshend would have produced is unknown. It is questionable as to whether the setting would have proved rich enough to provide a sufficient variety of subjects to nurture an extended stay. Quite probably his feelings for Vermont were in part the result of disintegrating health which had sapped him of the strength or the desire to seek greater challenges in his work.

Theodore Robinson's death at the age of forty-four did not occur at the conclusion of a lifetime of effort, but rather at the beginning of his artistic maturity. It is impossible to ascertain what future influences would have manifested themselves or in what manner his art would have progressed. Rather it is important to acknowledge what survives—a small body of canvases, not innovative, but extraordinarily truthful to his sensitive, poetic vision of nature.

Biography

THEODORE ROBINSON was born in Irasburg, Vermont, on 3 June 1852. With a characteristic bittersweet humor, he once commented on his origins:

My father was a farmer, and my grandparents were both very respectable and deserving domestic servants. I have never carried my investigation further up the family tree.[1]

Elijah Robinson was, in fact, a clergyman who, in 1856, shortly after Theodore's birth, moved his wife and children to Evansville, Wisconsin, where descendants of the family still reside.

Theodore Robinson began his formal art education in Chicago at the age of seventeen; however, asthma, the illness which was to plague him throughout his short life, soon forced him to Denver and, after a brief stay, home again to Evansville where he remained for four years. During this time, he apparently sketched local personages in order to accumulate enough funds to resume his artistic training in New York where he entered the school of the National Academy of Design in 1874.

Little is known of Robinson's activities during the next two years. Presumably he attended classes and acquainted himself with the broad art scene of this metropolitan center. He was evidently instrumental in the founding of the Art Students League, and his sketchbook of the period records glimpses of life throughout the city.

In 1876, he embarked on his first journey abroad, to France, traveling from Le Havre through the countryside of Normandy to Paris. Again, his sketchbooks serve to document his activity with their careful, somewhat restrained drawings of particularly interesting sights he found along the way.

The artistic climate of the French capital in the mid-1870's was one of debate over the Impressionists and their new, radical approach to painting. The young artist must have been

1. Harrison, p. 307

stirred by the controversy although at this time it had had no impact on the art scene in America, which was still devoted to the merits of the academies and the formalistic art they endorsed. Robinson, then following the lead of many of his compatriots, joined the atelier of the academician Carolus-Duran and shared a studio with a number of other Americans including Will H. Low, Birge Harrison, J. Carroll Beckwith, and John Singer Sargent.[2] In 1877, he apparently moved to Jean-Léon Gérôme's atelier at the Ecole des Beaux-Arts and briefly joined the classes of Benjamin Constant. The same year also marked the acceptance of his first painting by the Salon, a momentous occasion which he reported to his mother in a letter to Evansville: "My picture is accepted and I tremble with joy."[3] In the Summer of 1877, Robinson joined several of his fellow art students at Grez, near Fontainebleau, where there was a colony of English-speaking artists and writers. Among those present were Birge Harrison, Will H. Low, and Robert Louis Stevenson.[4]

After another year of study, Robinson left Paris for a stay in Italy. There in Venice, probably in Fall of 1879, he met James McNeill Whistler. Two souvenirs exist of their meeting: one, a painting by an unknown Italian artist with an inscription on the reverse indicating that it had been purchased jointly by Robinson and Whistler during their travels through the countryside; the other, a small oil sketch with Whistler's butterfly signature. The label on

JAMES McNEILL WHISTLER, *Oil Sketch*
Oil on Panel; 11¾ x 15 inches (frame size)
Inscribed lower left: *Venice / 1878*
Inscribed lower right:
To my friend Ford / Th. Robinson

Collection of Nevil Ford, New York

2. Baur, Brooklyn Museum, p. 15   3. Campbell, pp. 287-89
4. For a description of the art colony, see Harrison, p. 307ff.

the latter reads "Souvenir de Venice to Theodore Robinson from James McNeill Whistler."[5] Although the two never met again, Robinson's interest in the elder artist's activities remained constant, and his Diary frequently records humorous Whistlerian anecdotes.

His student days over, Robinson returned to America in late 1879 engaging a studio in New York. His finances depleted, however, by his European sojourn, he was forced to return to his home in Evansville early in 1880. Life in the rural mid-West proved to be a considerable departure from his cosmopolitan Parisian existence. Through his good friend Will H. Low, who had sensed from his letters the need "to extricate Robinson from his surroundings where . . . he was fast relapsing into a vegetable state,"[6] he obtained a teaching position at Mrs. Sylvanevus Reed's School in New York, returning to the city probably early in 1881.

He there joined a group of young men employed by the painter John LaFarge to work on mural decorations for both public and private buildings. The nature of the decorative style is indicated by Will Low's comment that the artists had "persuaded themselves for a year or so that the days of the Italian Renaissance were revived on Manhattan Island."[7] Indications are that Robinson was engaged in such work until late 1883, first for LaFarge and later for Prentice Treadwell for whom he probably worked on decorations for the then new Metropolitan Opera House. During this time, he also made a number of journeys from the city: to Jamaica, Vermont; Boston; and then to Nantucket where he summered with several other artists, including Joe Evans and Abbott Thayer, and produced a number of paintings of local subjects.

By the Spring of 1884, he had set aside enough money from his decorative work to return to France, spending the Summer of that year at Barbizon, a locale to which he returned on numerous occasions until 1887. Although Paris was essentially his permanent base during these years, he also made other excursions, notably to Holland in 1885 and to Dieppe in June of 1887. There are also indications of a number of short visits to New York.

Although Robinson had been in Giverny briefly in the Summer of 1887, it was not until 1888 that he "discovered" the village and its most notable resident, Claude Monet, who had settled there in May 1883. Will Low's description of the village and the surrounding countryside perhaps best indicates its character:

5. Both items are in the collection of Mr. Nevil Ford, New York. Although the oil sketch is dated 1878, it is likely that this was added at some later time as Whistler did not arrive in Venice until 1879.

6. Low, p. 283   7. Ibid., p. 285

Giverny, as a hamlet struggling along an unshaded road, offers at first glance little that is picturesque. Through the valley which it dominates runs the Seine, and between the village and the larger river winds a small stream, the Epte, with pleasantly shaded banks enclosed between broad meadows gracefully bordered by long lines of poplars. Its greatest charm lies in the atmospheric conditions over the lowlands, where the moisture from the rivers, imprisoned through the night by the valleys bordering hills, dissolve before the sun and bathe the landscape in an iridescent flood of vaporous hues. . . ." [8]

Within this setting with its soft mists and gentle landscape, the impressionistic tendencies which were already apparent in Robinson's art were matured, and he produced numerous canvases which blend light and color with direct realism.

Other artists in pursuit of the Impressionist master were also drawn to the village; however, Monet, covetous of his privacy, shunned virtually all, but evidence of his ensuing friendship with Robinson is plentiful. Curiously, where one would have expected a master-pupil relationship to evolve, such a connection was consistently denied by both. The countryside at Giverny and the artistic milieu of the village drew Robinson back each year through 1892. He generally remained there for the spring and summer months and spent the winters in New York.

Robinson received his first artistic award in 1890, the Webb Prize given at the annual exhibition of the Society of American Artists in New York to which he had been elected in 1881. The prize-winning work was his *Winter Landscape*, painted in December 1889, and its selection marked it as the first impressionist painting designated for the award.

The following winter, rather than returning to New York Robinson made his second journey to Italy. Although the specific reasons are somewhat obscure, it is probable that he sought a break in his usual routine, a refreshment of his eye and spirit. He painted several canvases at Capri before moving on to Frascati, near Rome, where he remained until March 1891. By April, he was back at Giverny for the summer. The trip had not been especially productive, and he recorded in his Diary, later after his return to New York, that his friend August Jaccaci, the art editor of *Scribner's* magazine, had "prodded me a little, said I had ought to have made better use of my Italian trip—made more typical and amusing things. . . . true enough. . . ." (4 April 1892)

8. Ibid., pp. 446-47

From December 1891 until May 1892, Robinson remained in New York except for a brief trip in March to Boston to hang an exhibition of his paintings, with those of Theodore Wendel, at the Williams and Everett Gallery. Late in April, shortly before his departure for France, he received his second public honor, the Shaw Fund Award for $1000 for his painting *In the Sun* 1891, a figurative canvas of a girl lying in the grass in a patch of bright sunlight.

In May, again at Giverny, he wrote enthusiastically to his friend J. Alden Weir:

I saw Monet Monday and a dozen or so canvases he did at Rouen last winter. They are the Cathedral, mostly the facade, filling up all the canvas, and they are simply colossal. Never, I believe has architecture been painted so before, the most astonishing impression of the thing, a feeling of size, grandeur and decay, an avoidance of the banal side of the subject. They are at all times of the day, one fog, and the tower gradually becomes less visible as the eye ascends. . . . Isn't it curious, a man taking such material and making such magnificent use of it. . . . Monet was cordiality, itself —It's very pleasant to think I have a place in his affection. [9]

This summer, his last at Giverny, was as the others had been. Days were spent painting or walking through the countryside with an occasional trip to Paris to see an exhibition or visit the Louvre. Frequently, aspiring young artists visited—mostly Americans drawn to the village by its ever-increasing fame as an art colony.

Robinson returned to America permanently in December, apparently having decided to devote himself to painting in his homeland. Although the reasons for the decision are never stated, it is likely that, for him, Giverny had served its purpose, and he now sought to apply his fully-developed impressionist style to the American scene.

Life in New York soon settled into a routine. A steady stream of friends and collectors, eager to see the results of his years of painting abroad, visited his studio at 11 East 14th Street, and his Diary is full of their comments and reactions to his work. In addition, young artists to whom he was now somewhat of a celebrity came to pay respectful calls. In a rather wistful tone, he recorded in his Diary one such visit:

Call from an admirer, a young art student. . . . It reminds me of my coming to New York and calling on Homer—only this boy has a confidence and ideas. Far ahead of mine at that time. (Diary, New York, 11 February 1893)

9. Young, p. 190

He also continued to send his work to the annual exhibitions of the Society of American Artists and the American Water Color Society as well as to shows at the National Academy of Design and the Pennsylvania Academy of the Fine Arts.

Robinson's return to America also revived close friendships with artists with whom he had formed associations in the 1870's and 1880's, in particular J. Alden Weir and John H. Twachtman. He was a frequent visitor to Twachtman's home in Greenwich, Connecticut, and also spent many long, enjoyable evenings at the Weirs' discussing art:

. . . dined with Weir and looked at a lot of Durers and others of his school. . . .
These are pleasant evenings—Weir's enthusiasm and criticism on things and the
pleasure of looking at good things with a friend, comparing impressions, etc.
(Diary, New York, 16 February 1893)

Although Robinson's moderate success resulted in the sale of a number of his canvases, he soon realized the necessity of deriving additional income from other sources, and, in Summer 1893, he took a teaching position, the first of several, in Napanoch, New York, on the Delaware and Hudson Canal. His students, all female, were pupils from New York art schools, and their activities were amusingly recorded in a contemporary journal:

The Delaware and Hudson Canal runs through the village, and the towpath bristles
with white umbrellas all day like a field with mushrooms after a fog. Parties board
the boats and are towed from one lock to another. The canal men are kindly inter-
ested in the progress of art and aid it when they can pointing out "the fresh greens"
and "tender purples" within sight. This artistic vernacular has become so common
that the very drivers stop their horses to point out "pretty bits" to the aspirants for
artistic glory.[10]

Of the instructor the article also reported:

Mr. Robinson consented after a good deal of entreaty, to be the guide of these would-
be impressionists. . . . In spite of being a devoted artist, Mr. Robinson is fortunately
gifted with a sense of humor which will carry him through the summer.[11]

Not accustomed to such a structured existence, Robinson found teaching difficult:

10. Unidentified newspaper clipping entitled "Women and Their Interests" provided through the courtesy of a private collector in Boston.
11. Ibid.

*My first month is over and it is hard work, especially as I've been a free man so long
—not teaching but doing just as I wanted. . . . There is some pleasure tho' in seeing
girls improve rapidly.* (Diary, Napanoch, 4 August 1893)

The summer months were not totally absorbed with teaching, however, and when the class
ended he remained at Napanoch until the end of October, working on a series of canvases
of scenic life along the canal. It was his initial attempt at painting impressionist works in
America, and he was not pleased with the results.

*I am afraid my American canvases will fall flat, it's a pity they are not completer—
some are good in intention, line or color, but none very complete except the evening . . . .*
(Diary, New York, 27 December 1893)

Robinson felt that he still had to discover in America the setting which would be suited to
his impressionistic style.

After a winter of considerable social activity but little actual work, Robinson's discovery of
the coastal town of Cos Cob, Connecticut, in June 1894, must have indeed been refreshing.
He had wearied of the pressures of city life and was eager to set up his easel and paint in the
open air. Obviously attracted by the qualities of light and color in the misty seaside atmosphere, he painted a small number of superb canvases dealing with nautical subjects. During
the Summer and Autumn 1894, he also spent considerable time in New Jersey, first, teaching
a month-long summer class at Evelyn College in Princeton, and then, painting and teaching
with Will Low in Brielle until his return to New York in mid-November.

The winter dragged and again for financial reasons he was forced to teach, taking over
Robert Vonnoh's classes at The Pennsylvania Academy of the Fine Arts which necessitated
his commuting to Philadelphia.

In February 1895, Robinson was given his first one-man show at the William Macbeth Gallery in New York. It consisted of forty-six works, the majority of which were paintings done
since his return to America. In general, the critics were favorable in their reviews of the exhibition, and, if a common theme prevailed throughout the notices, it was the observation
that Robinson was primarily a realist, recording nothing more than the vision before his eyes.
Characteristic of the reviews is this excerpt from a notice by Royal Cortissoz which appeared
in the *New York Tribune* on 3 February 1895 stating that the exhibition was

*tempting to describe as illustrative of the impressionism of Mr. Theodore Robinson,
rather than impressionism in general. . . . He has neither imagination nor sentiment,
and the spectator must therefore be content with a purely visual report of nature.*

That report is given, however, with such taste and skill, with such directness and
delicacy, that the absence of more subjective qualities is not suffered to spoil one's
pleasure in the work.

Unfortunately, the exhibition was not a financial success, and Robinson continued to be
plagued by his poor economic situation as well as by his failing health. Apprehensive about
his future, he made a special note of advice given him by Weir:

He thinks I ought to have a place of my own and get acquainted with it—grow up
with it. I must think of this—Cos Cob, perhaps. (Diary, New York, 11 April 1895)

Although the Connecticut shore was for him an ideal setting in an artistic sense, it was
the place of his birth which would ultimately provide him with the "place of his own" for
which he had been searching since his return from France.

After a number of day-long painting excursions to Haverstraw on the Hudson River where
he managed to paint a small number of landscapes which are interesting in their surprisingly
abstract quality, he set out in mid-May of 1895 for Townshend, Vermont, where relatives of
his mother maintained a house. The Cheneys, "Cousin Agnes" and her two daughters, Alice
and Helen, provided him with an enormous sense of warmth and family spirit, feelings which
he had not experienced since leaving Evansville in 1881. His Diary for the period abounds in
the reporting of familial trivia, as he submerged himself into this welcome existence.

As the summer progressed, Robinson became acquainted with the Vermont landscape, its
gently rolling hills and broad valleys. Although Robinson's health was failing and the time
proved to be an unproductive period artistically, he had indeed found a "place of his own."
This feeling was conveyed to his friend August Jaccaci whose comment he recorded in
his Diary:

One [a letter] *from Jaccaci—he thinks my letters indicate that I have found a country*
in America that charms as much or almost as much as certain parts of France, he is
glad to hear it. . . . (Townshend, 1 October 1895)

Robinson felt that he had wasted time at Townshend, but he resolved to return the following summer and also for a few weeks during the winter with the hope of painting enough
canvases to have an exhibition of his work the next year. In November 1895, he went back to
New York. However, his plans and aspirations were never to be realized. Theodore Robinson
died on 2 April 1896 during an acute asthma attack in Agnes Cheney's West 55th Street apart-
ment at the tragically young age of forty-four.

THEODORE ROBINSON (seated)
Courtesy of Ira Spanierman, Inc.

I. Paintings and Watercolors

The most comprehensive study of Theodore Robinson's work to date is John I. H. Baur's monograph *Theodore Robinson 1852-1896* (New York: The Brooklyn Museum, 1946). Reference numbers cited in the catalogue entries are from Baur's listing of Robinson's works.

The extant volumes of Theodore Robinson's Diary for 1892-96 are in the collection of the Frick Art Reference Library, New York. Passages from the Diary which are used in the text of this catalogue have been quoted directly.

For practical reasons, bibliographical references in the catalogue entries are shortened. Exhibitions are listed by year and institution or organization which held the exhibition, for example, ''1946, Brooklyn Museum.'' Other references are listed by author's last name, when a specific author is given, or by the title of the publication in shortened form. The more complete reference is given in the Selected Bibliography at the end of the book where exhibition catalogues are found under the institution's name, arranged alphabetically, and, within that category, chronologically; other references are listed separately and arranged alphabetically.

1

ROUEN CATHEDRAL ca. 1876

Oil on canvas; 17¾ x 11¾ inches
Inscription on back: *From / Th. Ro[. . .]son / for*

Provenance: Mrs. Agnes McCahill; Miss Frances Del Mar, New York; Mrs. Paul Blackwelder, St. Louis; Florence Lewison Gallery, New York

Exhibitions: 1962, Florence Lewison Gallery, no. 13; 1971, Southern Vermont Artists, no. 14

Bibliography: Baur, Brooklyn Museum, pp. 74-75; *Robinson,* Kennedy Galleries, p. 9

Owner: Mr. and Mrs. Paul Landau, New York

The crowded narrow streets of Rouen with their Norman buildings appealed to the young Robinson on his first European trip in 1876. Similar urban vistas appear in his sketchbook of this period in detailed, finished studies (see fig. a), and there is an oil on paper, *Houses at Rouen* (Baur, no. 101; *Robinson,* Kennedy Galleries, repro. p. 17) which probably dates from the same year.

In the canvas, he has successfully contrasted the richly ornamented Gothic facade of Rouen Cathedral with the geometric forms of the secular architecture which are heightened by the play of light and shadow.

2

FRENCH FACADE

Oil on canvas; 15½ x 10½ inches
Unsigned

Provenance: Alice Cheney, Townshend, Vermont,
from the artist

Owner: Private Collection, Boston

The heavy impasto, vertical format and strong
contrasts of sunlight and shadow in this painting
are reminiscent of Robinson's works executed
during his first stay abroad from 1876 to 1879
(for comparison, see *Rouen Cathedral,* cat. no.
1; *Man on Rocks,* Baur, no. 142). There is a
nearly identical watercolor (see 1964-66,
American Federation of Arts, no. 61) with the
inscription, *Vieilles maisons—Clamart / Th.
Robinson—1883,* suggesting a similar date for
the painting, however, Robinson was in America
at this time. It is most likely that the inscription
was added at a later date by someone other than
the artist.

3

KITCHEN INTERIOR ca. 1880

Oil on canvas; 9½ x 14¼ inches
Inscription on back: *TH. ROBINSON*

Provenance: Mrs. Agnes McCahill, Miss Frances Del Mar, New York; Mrs. Paul Blackwelder, St. Louis; Florence Lewison Gallery, New York

Exhibitions: 1962, Florence Lewison Gallery, no. 14; 1971, Southern Vermont Artists, no. 15

Bibliography: Baur, Brooklyn Museum, p. 67

Owner: Mr. and Mrs. Paul Landau, New York

Robinson's years of formal study abroad ended with his return to America late in 1879. Probably for financial reasons, he spent most of 1880 with his family in Evansville, Wisconsin, and it is likely that he painted this charming kitchen scene there. Its oblique viewpoint and dramatic play of light are features it shares with another domestic interior, *Woman Weaving* (Baur, no. 269; *Robinson*, Kennedy Galleries, repro. p. 16) which has been dated from the same period. In the studied arrangement of objects and their sensitive rendering, this painting comes closer to pure still life than any other in Robinson's oeuvre.

4

BARBIZON 1885

Oil on canvas; 7½ x 11¾ inches
Signed lower left: *TH. ROBINSON*
Inscribed and dated lower right: *BARBIZON / '85*

Owner: Kennedy Galleries, Inc., New York

Although settled in Paris between 1884 and 1888, Robinson, an admirer of Corot, Daubigny and other Barbizon painters, made periodic excursions into the surrounding countryside. The plains of Barbizon are depicted here in alternating broad bands of grayed-greens and browns which recede to the strip of brilliant blue at the horizon with its suggestion of village architecture. The sense of depth is further accentuated by the road which meanders back through the rain-washed fields.

5

MACHERIN 1885

Oil on canvas; 10½ x 16 inches
Signed and dated lower right: *TH-ROBINSON-1885*
Inscribed lower left: *MACHERIN*

Provenance: J. M. Lichtenauer; Mrs. William
Bridges Thayer

Exhibitions: 1946, Brooklyn Museum, no. 139,
pl. iii; 1964, University of Wisconsin, no. 7

Bibliography: Robinson, Kennedy Galleries, p. 11

Owner: University of Kansas Museum of Art,
Lawrence, Kansas
William Bridges Thayer Memorial

Similar to the view of Barbizon (cat. no. 4) is
this landscape also dated 1885 and inscribed
with the name of the Dutch town, Macherin
(Macheren). If, in fact, this serves as an
indication of a journey to Holland, it must
have been of short duration as no other
documentation exists.

6

A COBBLER OF OLD PARIS (COBBLER SHOP) 1885

Oil on canvas; 25½ x 20½ inches
Signed and dated lower right: *Th Robinson / 1885*

Provenance: Duncan Phillips; Phillips *et al* Sale, American Art Assoc., New York, 27 February 1922, no. 30, repro.; M. Knoedler and Co., New York, 1923

Exhibitions: 1886, Inter-State Industrial Exposition of Chicago, no. 97

Bibliography: Baur, Brooklyn Museum, pp. 25 & 60, pl. ii; *Robinson,* Kennedy Galleries, p. 11; *Catalogue,* Smith College, p. 8

Owner: Smith College Museum of Art, Northampton, Massachusetts

Dark tonalities and a somewhat sombre mood characterize many of Robinson's paintings of the period, 1884-87. It seems to have been a time of experimentation and of a certain indecisiveness in his art. Having resolved to leave the employ of the popular decorative painters, John LaFarge and Prentice Treadwell for whom he worked off and on from 1881-83, it is as though he had to redefine, for himself, his position as an easel painter.

This rather solemn, firmly-painted canvas of a cobbler working at his bench in front of an open window seems to echo elements of the northern Dutch genre, further indicating the possibility of a trip to Holland.

7

GIRL IN A RED DRESS 1885

Watercolor; 5½ x 13 inches
Signed and dated upper left: *T. Robinson / Paris '85*

Provenance: John F. Braun; Mr. and Mrs. Lawrence Fleischman, Detroit; Mr. and Mrs. Irving F. Burton, Huntington Woods, Michigan

Exhibitions: 1961, John Herron Art Museum; 1961, Institute of Arts, Michigan; 1962, Detroit Institute of Arts

Bibliography: Baur, Brooklyn Museum, p. 84

Owner: Mann Galleries, Miami, Florida

The delicate hues of the face and the neck of the young girl together with the rather strong red of her dress are in contrast to the mottled foliage which surrounds her. Although quite intimate in feeling, there is a certain monumentality in the watercolor which is evident in other figurative paintings of the period. They would seem, as Baur points out in his monograph (p. 26), to bear a relationship to the decorative murals on which Robinson worked under La-Farge and Treadwell. There is an oil version (Private Collection, New York) of this watercolor which is undated but nearly identical in size as well as in the suggestion of such details as the quadrants in the corners which are purely decorative elements.

8

GIRL SEATED, WRITING ca. 1885

Oil on canvas; 25 x 20 inches
Inscription lower right: *Th. Robinson / H. E. Robinson / Apr*

Provenance: Mrs. Agnes McCahill; Miss Frances Del Mar, New York; Mrs. Paul Blackwelder, St. Louis; Florence Lewison Gallery, New York

Exhibitions: 1962, Florence Lewison Gallery, no. 3, repro; 1965, Florence Lewison Gallery, no. 14, repro. on cover

Bibliography: Baur, Brooklyn Museum, pp. 63-64; *Robinson,* Kennedy Galleries, p. 11

Owner: Mr. and Mrs. Maurice Glickman, New York

This work once again recalls the romantic, decorative style of the architectural murals on which Robinson was engaged while in the employ of LaFarge and Treadwell. The girl, her clothing almost medieval in feeling, gazes at the viewer with a trance-like stare. She sits in tall grass, and the wispy quality of its brushstroke is in contrast to the solid, sculptural folds of her dress. The articulation of the foliage surrounding the figure resembles that of the watercolor *Girl in a Red Dress* (cat. no. 7) and its related oil, thus indicating a similar date. Baur (p. 44) has suggested that monochromes such as this, of which Robinson did several, represent his manner of adapting his art to a reproductive medium for use as illustrative material in contemporary journals.

The inscription on this painting was most likely added by Hamline Robinson after his brother's death.

9

THE CABBAGE PATCH ca. 1885

Oil on canvas; 14 x 9⅝ inches
Signed lower right: *TH. ROBINSON*

Provenance: Edwin S. Chapin; Mrs. Edwin Chapin,
New York; Florence Lewison Gallery, New York

Exhibitions: 1946, Brooklyn Museum, no. 31; 1962,
Florence Lewison Gallery, no. 16; 1963, IBM, no. 46;
1972, Whitney Museum of American Art, no. 60

Bibliography: Lewison, p. 72; *Robinson,* Kennedy
Galleries, p. 11; *Illustrated Sales Catalogue,* Bunn
et al Sale, p. 188 (as *A Brittany Farm*)

Owner: Mr. and Mrs. Raymond J. Horowitz, New York

Inscribed on the reverse of this painting
by a previous owner, Edwin S. Chapin, is *The
Cabbage Patch | Painted at Giverny, France |
in 1887.* However, the work closely resembles
another canvas of the same subject (Baur, no.
30) which is signed and dated 1885, thus suggesting an earlier date and a location other than
Giverny. The principal difference in the two
works is the omission of the peasant woman in
the dated version. In this canvas, Robinson
has employed the device of the high horizon in
order to emphasize the lush vegetation of the
foreground.

Fig. a
Photograph for
Poppy Field
9¾ x 7¼ inches
Courtesy of
Ira Spanierman, Inc.,
New York

Bibliography: Lewison, p. 72; *Robinson*, Kennedy Galleries, p. 11

Owner: Florence Lewison Gallery, New York

10

POPPY FIELD *(*FIELD OF POPPIES*)* ca. 1885

Oil on canvas; 20⅛ x 16¼ inches
Signed lower right (blurred): *TH. ROBINSON*

Provenance: Mrs. Agnes McCahill, Miss Frances Del Mar, New York; Mrs. Paul Blackwelder, St. Louis

Exhibitions: 1946, Brooklyn Museum, no. 182; 1962, Florence Lewison Gallery, no. 9; 1965, University of New Mexico Art Gallery, no. 47, repro. p. 47; 1971, Southern Vermont Artists, no. 13

This would appear to be the only pure landscape which had is origins in a photograph (fig. a), and both the photograph and the painted version are remarkable in the images they present. Robinson, the photographer, has positioned his camera in the tangled mass of a field of poppies, recording, in minute detail, the fragile forms of the flowers in contrast to the linear shafts of grain. In the painting, he has greatly simplified these elements, choosing to emphasize, instead, a sense of enormous depth. Once again, he has accomplished this by accentuating the high horizon, only barely visible in the photograph. Robinson, as he does in several of his works based on photographs, has faithfully transferred to the canvas an imperfection seen in the photograph—the light-struck area in the foreground.

11

RIVER LANDSCAPE

Oil on canvas; 9½ x 15½ inches
Signed lower right: *Th. Robinson*
Inscribed lower left: *To Cousin Alice with best wishes*

Provenance: Alice Cheney, Townshend, Vermont,
from the artist

Owner: Private Collection, Boston

This tranquil river view with its subtle tonalities is one of Robinson's most lyrical paintings. The high horizon, the subdued colors and the dry brushstroke suggest that the canvas dates from his Barbizon period in the mid-1880's, prior to his discovery of Giverny. The discrepancy in script between the signature at the lower right and the inscription at the lower left would seem to indicate that the artist presented the painting to his cousin a number of years after its completion, possibly during his summer in Vermont in 1895. There is another view, quite similar in feeling, entitled *French Farm House* (Private Collection, Boston) which bears the inscription, *To Cousin Helen with best wishes.*

12

MOTHER AND CHILD

Oil on canvas; 23 x 18 inches
Unsigned

Provenance: Robinson Estate Sale, American Art
Assoc., New York, 24 March 1898, no. 9; Moses H.
Cone for Etta Cone, Baltimore

Bibliography: Cone Collection, 1934, p. 26; Baur,
Brooklyn Museum, pp. 69-70; Pollack, p. 34

Owner: The Baltimore Museum of Art;
Cone Collection

The mottled patterning and suggestion of
filtered light superimposed on the sombre
Barbizon tonalities of olive green, brown, and
tan indicate that this canvas may be a transitional work dating from the mid-1880's when
Robinson was engaged in early, tentative
explorations of impressionist techniques.

13

GIRL WITH A GOAT 1886

Oil on canvas; 16 x 11 inches
Signed and dated lower right: *TH. ROBINSON / 1886*

Owner: Steven Straw Company, Seabrook,
New Hampshire

Although Robinson did not meet Claude
Monet in the village of Giverny until 1888,
it is evident in many of his canvases of the mid-
1880's that he was already absorbed by some of
the techniques of Impressionism at this time.
Here, a peasant woman pauses for a moment in
the brilliant sunlight as she leads her goat
through a doorway. Pastel tones, indicating
reflected color from the surroundings, flicker
across the surface of the stone and the fabric
of her dress. The atmosphere shimmers in the
heat of a summer day, and it is clear that the
final step to Impressionism would be a very
short one indeed.

14

GIRL LYING IN GRASS 1886

Watercolor; 5½ x 10 inches
Signed and dated upper right: *Th. Robinson/'86*

Provenance: Edwin Ford, from the artist; Nevil Ford, New York

Bibliography: Baur, Brooklyn Museum, p. 84

Owner: Colby College Art Museum, Waterville, Maine

The degree of Robinson's adherence to a preliminary photographic study varies from work to work. It is evident here that the figures are directly related and, in both versions, are essentially similiar in value relationships although the contrasts in the photograph are more pronounced. Instead of placing the girl against the rocky background, however, Robinson has moved her to a field of poppies, which is reminiscent of his canvas *Poppy Field* (cat. no. 10).

In the Sun (see Baur, no. 115), an oil of 1891, also represents a model reclining in a grassy field. It, too, depends on a photograph, but as the model appears to be different and the date of the oil is considerably later, it is likely that they bear no direct relationship to this watercolor and its preliminary photographic study.

Fig. a
Photograph for
Girl Lying in Grass
4¹/₁₆ x 9½ inches
Courtesy of
Ira Spanierman, Inc.,
New York

15

At the Piano 1887

Oil on canvas; 16¼ x 26 inches
Signed, inscribed and dated lower right: *Th. Robinson, Paris / 1887*

Provenance: Robinson Estate Sale, American Art Assoc., New York, 24 March 1898, no. 21; C. Armstrong; Sidney Curtis, 1928; Macbeth Gallery, New York, 1928; Milch Gallery, New York; John Gellatly, New York

Bibliography: Baur, Brooklyn Museum, pp. 25 & 57-58, pl. v; *Robinson,* Kennedy Galleries, p. 11

Owner: National Collection of Fine Arts, Smithsonian Institution, Washington, D. C.

(To be exhibited in Baltimore only)

A young girl sits practicing her piano lessons in this canvas painted in France in 1887. Superficially, it would seem to bear a certain relationship to James McNeill Whistler's work also entitled *At The Piano* (begun 1858; Collection, Cincinnati Art Museum) in its subject matter, carefully arranged composition, and in the feeling of serenity which it evokes. It is conceivable that Robinson may have seen Whistler's painting when it was exhibited in this country—first at the Pennsylvania Academy of the Fine Arts, Philadelphia, in 1881 and later at the Society of American Artists, New York, in 1882. While Whistler's canvas is ponderous with its cluttered space and dark masses, Robinson's interior, bathed in a gentle light, is airy and unencumbered.

16

GIRL AT PIANO ca. 1887

Oil on canvas; 24½ x 20½ inches
Signed lower left: *Th. Robinson*

Provenance: Robinson Estate Sale, American Art
Assoc., New York, 24 March 1898, no. 85

Exhibitions: 1910, Königliche Akademie der Kunste,
p. 71, repro.; 1915, Reading Public Museum; 1946,
Brooklyn Museum, no. 74

Bibliography: Levy, pp. 11-12; *Robinson*, Kennedy
Galleries, p. 11

Owner: The Pennsylvania Academy of the Fine Arts,
Philadelphia; Gilpin Fund Purchase, 1898

In this canvas, probably dating from the late
1880's, Robinson has eliminated all superfluous
elements in order to emphasize the main theme
of the girl, intent on her music. Through the use
of a strong single light-source and the careful
articulation of certain selected details, he has
accentuated the central passage of the painting—
the profile of the figure, her hands on the key-
board and the sheet of notes from which she reads.

On 23 February 1893 in New York, Robinson
noted in his Diary that *Girl at Piano,* then on
view in a loan exhibition, possibly at the Society
of American Artists in New York, "looks well,
is naive and personal." The entry continues in
a broader vein, however, critical of the obvious
severity of this painting and others:

*My painting is good as far as it goes but I have
confused simplicity with other qualities, and it is
apt to be rather poor, not full or rich enough in
vocabulary, like my writing.*

There is another painting based on the theme
of a young girl at the piano (see Baur, no. 120).

17

PORTRAIT OF WILL H. LOW

Oil on canvas; 21 x 17 inches
Unsigned

Provenance: Will H. Low, New York

Exhibitions: 1935, National Academy of Design;
1964, University of Wisconsin, no. 24

Bibliography: Baur, Brooklyn Museum, p. 73

Owner: National Academy of Design, New York

Will H. Low (1853-1932) and Robinson's
association began in Paris in the mid-1870's
when they were students together at the ateliers
of Carolus-Duran and Gérôme. As an illustrator
and decorator, Low's art catered to the popular
tastes of the time, and his murals and ceiling
decorations could be found in many homes in
the New York City area, as well as in the Plaza
and the Waldorf-Astoria Hotels.

The bonds of friendship between the two men
were strong and enduring. It was with Low and
his wife that Robinson often shared the more
personal aspects of his life, and Low's touching
references to his friend in his *Chronicle of
Friendships* testify to their closeness.

Portraits by Robinson are virtually non-existent,
yet he felt compelled to do a study of Low, and
one senses, in this sketchy, unresolved canvas,
the struggle to reconcile the man whom he knew
and admired with what he felt were the dictates
of formal portraiture in the late nineteenth
century. Low presented this portrait to the
National Academy of Design in 1888, the year
of his election to that institution.

18

THE YOUNG VIOLINIST

Oil on canvas; 32 x 26 inches
Unsigned

Provenance: Theodore Robinson Estate Sale,
American Art Assoc., New York, 24 March 1898,
no. 34; Moses H. Cone for Etta Cone, Baltimore

Bibliography: Cone Collection, 1934, p. 26; Baur,
Brooklyn Museum, p. 82; *The Cone Collection,* 1967,
p. 68; Pollack, p. 34

Owner: The Baltimore Museum of Art,
Cone Collection

A young girl, her dress spotted with sunlight,
walks in a tree-shaded grove, absorbed in tuning
her violin. The gentle yet unconventional color
together with the firm, diagonal brushstrokes
give atmosphere and a sense of movement to the
canvas, revealing Robinson's broad, impressionistic style of the late 1880's.

19

IN THE GROVE (GIRL IN WOODS) ca. 1888

Oil on canvas; 32 x 26 inches
Unsigned

Provenance: Robinson Estate Sale, American Art
Assoc., New York, 24 March 1898, no. 37; Moses H.
Cone for Etta Cone, Baltimore

Exhibitions: 1946, Brooklyn Museum, no. 108; 1958,
Woman's College, University of North Carolina; 1959,
American Academy and National Institue of Arts
and Letters

Bibliography: Cone Collection, 1934, p. 26, pl. 22;
The Cone Collection, 1967, p. 68; Baur, Brooklyn
Museum, p. 26; Pollack, p. 34; *Robinson,* Kennedy
Galleries, p. 12

Owner: The Baltimore Museum of Art,
Cone Collection

20

LA VACHÈRE (GIRL AND COW) 1888

Oil on canvas; 86¾ x 61½ inches
Signed and dated lower left: *TH. ROBINSON 1888*

Provenance: William T. Evans, New York, 1906;
Metropolitan Museum of Art, New York; Babcock
Galleries, New York; Joseph Katz, Baltimore

Exhibitions: 1889, Salon, Paris, no. 2306; 1889, Inter-
State Industrial Exposition of Chicago, no. 364; 1946,
Brooklyn Museum, no. 234, pl. x; 1959, American
Academy and National Institute of Arts and Letters

Bibliography: Levy, pp. 111-12, repro.; Burroughs,
p. 306; Baur, Brooklyn Museum, p. 26; *Robinson,*
Kennedy Galleries, p. 12; Truettner, p. 77

Owner: The Baltimore Museum of Art
Gift in Memory of Joseph Katz from His Children

The theme of the young peasant girl sewing as she tends her cows seems to have been of special interest to Robinson, for it appears frequently in his oeuvre. He also chose to immortalize her in rather sentimental verse in his only published poem which appeared in *Scribner's Magazine* in June 1897. Certainly the most monumental of all the representations is this large canvas painted in 1888, during his first summer at Giverny with Monet, which demonstrates the nature of his initial involvement with the techniques of French Impressionism.

Various shades of pink predominate in the essentially naturalistic rendering of the girl and cow, standing in a grove of trees that shimmer in reflected light. The individual forms of the leaves are mixed tones of primarily blue and green, thickly applied to the pink-primed canvas. Shadows in colorful, yet muted tones, give form to the figure and gently articulate her sensitive face. She seems curiously oblivious to the cow whose stolid presence challenges her dominance in the painting.

There is a nearly identical canvas, although considerably smaller, probably predating this work (see *La Vachère*, Baur, no. 235). *In the Grove* (cat. no. 19) in which the cow does not appear is yet another version. It is considerably lower in key with less range in color. Interesting to note are the faint traces of a transfer grid on this canvas, as well as the large *La Vachère*, suggesting the possibility that *In the Grove* may have been used as the preliminary study. In addition, oil sketches for the head of the cow (Baur, no. 236) and for the girl's head exist (Baur, no. 237), which are directly related to the final dated version.

21

DECORATIVE HEAD 1889

Watercolor; 14 x 10 inches
Signed and dated lower center: — *TH. ROBINSON -- 89*

Provenance: T. Gilbert Brouillette, 1937; Macbeth Gallery, New York, 1939

Exhibitions: 1889, American Water Color Society, no. 771; 1889, Inter-State Industrial Exposition of Chicago, no. 367; 1890, Boston Art Club, no. 219; 1939, Macbeth Gallery, no. 63; 1942, Whitney Museum of American Art, no. 124; 1946, Brooklyn Museum, no. 290, pl. xi; 1960, Charles E. Slatkin Galleries, no. 6

Bibliography: Baur, Brooklyn Museum, pp. 26 & 28; *Robinson*, Kennedy Galleries, p. 12

Owner: The Brooklyn Museum, New York

The size of this watercolor and the trace of a grid would seem to indicate that Robinson copied the head directly from his large *La Vachère* of 1888 (cat. no. 20). The trunks of the trees in the upper left suggesting depth, the light background framing the profile, and the pattern of the highlights and shadows on the head and neck are all elements faithfully transferred. Yet this watercolor, freer and infinitely softer, is perhaps the most beautiful version of all.

22

VAL D'ARCONVILLE ca. 1888

Oil on canvas; 18 x 21⅞ inches
Signed lower right: *TH. ROBINSON*

Provenance: Arthur A. Carey from the artist; M.
Knoedler and Co., New York, 1908; Hillyer Art
Gallery, Smith College, Northampton; M. Knoedler
and Co., New York; Mrs. Harold Hambidge Warner

Exhibitions: 1889, Society of American Artists,
no. 119; 1915, Panama-Pacific International Exposition,
no. 2668; 1939, Museum of Modern Art Gallery,
Washington, D. C.; 1940, Los Angeles County
Museum, no. 76; 1946, Brooklyn Museum, no. 238,
pl. ix; 1964, University of Wisconsin, no. 11; 1966,
Kennedy Galleries, no. 41, repro. p. 31

*Bibliography: Paintings in the Art Institute of
Chicago,* p. 402; *Robinson,* Kennedy Galleries, p. 12;
Hoopes, pp. 48-49, repro. p. 49;

Owner: The Art Institute of Chicago

Dating from his early years at Giverny and his
contacts with Monet, *Val d'Arconville* is one
of Robinson's freshest impressionistic canvases.
Marie, a girl for whom he had a strong romantic
attachment (see Baur, pp. 24-25) sits on a flower-
filled hillside above the houses at Arconville
and the rural countryside beyond. This sweeping
view of the Seine valley with its continual variations in color and light is a vista to which
the artist returned frequently.

Robinson used the theme of the figure seated in
the landscape in a number of other works including *On the Cliff* (Baur, no. 170), a small
oil painted at Dieppe in June 1887; a pastel of
the same title (Baur, no. 340), dated ca. 1887;
as well as in an oil dated 1891 (Baur, no. 198)
and a pastel (Baur, no. 341) both entitled
La Roche-Guyon.

23

BIRD'S EYE VIEW: GIVERNY, FRANCE 1889

Oil on canvas; 26 x 32½ inches
Signed and dated lower left: *TH. ROBINSON - 1889*

Provenance: Robinson Estate Sale, American Art Assoc., New York, 24 March 1898, no. 91; George A. Hearn, New York

Exhibitions: 1890, Society of American Artists, no. 152; 1890, Inter-State Industrial Exposition of Chicago, no. 249; 1891, Pennsylvania Academy, no. 250; 1892, Boston Art Club, no. 134; 1895, Macbeth Gallery, no. 21; 1895, Cotton States and International Exposition, no. 502; 1896, Chicago Society of Artists, no. 65; 1896, St. Louis Museum, no. 18; 1897, Cincinnati Museum Association, no. 16; 1935, Union League Club, no. 23; 1964, University of Iowa, no. 45; 1970, Metropolitan Museum, no. 186, repro.

Bibliography: Catalogue, Hearn Collection, 1908 no. 217, repro.; Burroughs, p. 306; Baur, Brooklyn Museum, pp. 29 & 58; Lewison, p. 72; *Robinson,* Kennedy Galleries, p. 12; Hoopes, pp. 50-51, repro. p. 51

Owner: The Metropolitan Museum of Art, New York, Gift of George A. Hearn, 1910

The village of Giverny in the Seine valley located northwest of Paris became a gathering place for American artists after Monet settled there in 1883. Here, from high on the hillside steeply rising above the village, Robinson depicted the stark rural architecture in block-like fashion with the landscape of the valley stretching beyond. The plowed, barren field on the right, the absence of foliage, and the hazy muted tones suggest that this is an autumnal view.

24

GIVERNY ca. 1889

Oil on canvas; 15½ x 22 inches
Unsigned

Exhibitions: 1931, Newark Museum; 1944, Phillips
Memorial Gallery, no. 17

Bibliography: Phillips, p. 107; Baur, Brooklyn
Museum, p. 64; *Phillips Collection Catalogue,* p. 85;
Robinson, Kennedy Galleries, p. 12

Owner: The Phillips Collection, Washington, D. C.

Although similar to the view of Giverny in
the Metropolitan Museum of Art (cat. no. 23)
the sense of space is less panoramic in this
canvas, and it is obvious that it was painted from
a lower vantage point, possibly the terrace of the
Hotel Baudy, situated above the village, where
Robinson lived during most of his stays at
Giverny. Less precisely painted than the Metropolitan Museum version, and higher in key, it
is one of a number of similar views executed
during his years at Giverny from 1887-92.

25

MOYEN AGE 1889

Watercolor; 14 x 10 inches
Signed and dated lower right: *18 Th. Robinson '89*

Provenance: Hamline Robinson, from the artist;
Mrs. C. F. Terhune, Kansas City, Missouri; Kennedy
Galleries, New York

Exhibitions: 1889, American Water Color Society, no.
772; 1946, Brooklyn Museum, no. 309; 1966, Kennedy
Galleries, no. 31, repro. p. 28

Bibliography: Baur, Brooklyn Museum, p. 29; *Robinson,* Kennedy Galleries, p. 12

Owner: Chapellier Galleries, New York

The setting and the date of this watercolor
suggest that it was painted in Giverny. It is a
curious work, the figure of the melancholy girl
in her medieval, hooded dress, an echo of his
romantic decorative style of the early 1880's.
Yet she is superimposed upon his beloved Seine
landscape with its soft blues, mauves, and
greens. The technique is tight; the brushstrokes
are small and seemingly ill-suited to a medium
which is meant to flow.

Although exhibited in the American Water
Color Society Exhibition of 1889, an entry made
in his Diary on January 29, 1893 suggests, as does
the rather labored quality of the watercolor, that
he was still working on *Moyen Age* four
years later.

26

NORMANDY CIDER MILL ca. 1889

Oil on canvas; 18½ x 15 inches
Signed lower left: *Th. Robinson*

Provenance: Ainslie Gallery, New York; Dr. Hyatt
Lyke; LeRoy Ireland, New York; Kennedy Galleries,
New York

Exhibitions: 1890, National Academy of Design,
no. 44; 1891, Pennsylvania Academy, no. 253; 1946,
Brooklyn Museum, no. 154

Bibliography: Robinson, Kennedy Galleries, p. 12

Owner: Private Collection, New York

The mechanism of the cider mill with its
complexity of forms is the dominant feature in
this painting probably dating from the latter
part of 1889. Soft gray-greens, tans and browns
are brushed on in a variety of strokes, some bold,
others blended one into the other. Stronger, warm
colors highlight the edges of some of the forms
giving a certain glow to the painting. The jug
in the foreground rendered in rich orange
tonalities completes this carefully constructed
canvas.

27

ETUDE 1890

Oil on canvas; 12 x 16¼ inches
Signed, inscribed and dated lower left: *Th. Robinson / Paris 1890*

Provenance: Edwin S. Chapin; Mrs. Edwin S. Chapin, New York; Harry Shaw Newman Gallery, New York; Dr. Seymour Wadler, New York; Florence Lewison Gallery, New York

Exhibitions: 1892, Union League Club, no. 54; 1946, Brooklyn Museum, no. 59, pl. xvi; 1971, Southern Vermont Artists, no. 8, repro. on cover

Bibliography: Robinson, Kennedy Galleries, p. 13

Owner: Mr. and Mrs. Raymond J. Horowitz, New York

Frequently, Robinson returned to the subject of the peasant woman, portraying her in familiar surroundings. In general, these are intimate glimpses of life, many perhaps posed and seemingly static in quality, but still essentially genre views. In this canvas, he has imbued his subject with a sense of nobility, stressing, through the austere simplicity of the composition, her relationship to the soil.

The inscription and date on the work would seem to indicate that it was not painted on the site but rather in a Paris studio. This is corroborated by the following information which appears on a label on the reverse:

Normandy Peasant Girl 12 x 16. Painted in Paris—1890. The figure is Mimi, his favorite model. Mrs. Lumsden (his pupil) saw him paint it . . .

28

LANDSCAPE AT AUVERS 1890

Oil on canvas mounted on board; 13¼ x 19¼ inches
Inscribed lower right: *To My friend | Friedlander |
H | | WP*
Inscribed and dated lower left: *Auvers —May .90*

Provenance: Friedlander; Richard L. Mills, Exeter,
New Hampshire

Owner: Mr. and Mrs. William Young, Wellesley Hills,
Massachusetts

(To be exhibited in Baltimore only)

Previously unrecorded in Robinson's oeuvre, this landscape is of considerable importance due to its informative inscriptions. The letters, *H/ /WP*, in the lower right-hand corner undoubtedly stand for Holder/Webb Prize, an honor which was awarded to the artist in the Spring of 1890 for his canvas, *A Winter Landscape* (Baur, no. 264). Given at the annual exhibition of the Society of American Artists, the prize, established in 1887, was presented "for the best landscape in the exhibition painted by an American artist under forty years of age" (Baur, p. 29). Obviously pleased at the distinction, Robinson used the letters as a pseudonym. Of further interest is the identification of the site as Auvers, since it is the only indication that the artist visited this small town northwest of Paris.

Photographic studies for
The Watering Pots and *At the Fountain*
Fig. a   7⅝ x 3¼ inches
Fig. b   7¼ x 5⅜ inches
Courtesy of
Ira Spanierman, Inc., New York

29

THE WATERING POTS 1890

Oil on canvas; 22 by 18⅛ inches
Signed and dated lower right: *Th. Robinson / 1890*

Provenance: Frank L. Babbott from the artist, 1893;
Edward G. O'Reilly; O'Reilly *et al* Sale, American Art
Assoc., New York, 24 January 1917, no. 53; John
S. Radway

Exhibitions: 1890, National Academy of Design, no.
586; 1890, Inter-State Industrial Exposition of
Chicago, no. 250; 1891, Pennsylvania Academy, no.
251; 1892, Boston Art Club, no. 111; 1892, Williams
and Everett Gallery, no. 45; 1932, Brooklyn Museum,
no. 81; 1946, Brooklyn Museum, no. 254, pl. xiv;
1971, Southern Vermont Artists, no. 1

Bibliography: Baur, Brooklyn Museum, pp. 28 & 31;
Robinson, Kennedy Galleries, p. 13; Hoopes, pp. 52-53,
repro. p. 53

Owner: The Brooklyn Museum, New York

30

At the Fountain (Josephine in the Garden)
ca. 1890

Oil on canvas; 32 x 26 inches
Unsigned

Provenance: Robinson Estate Sale, American Art
Assoc., New York, 24 March 1898, no. 36; George D.
Pratt; John Levy Gallery, New York, 1946; Macbeth
Gallery, New York, 1946

Exhibitions: 1946, Brooklyn Museum, no. 9, pl. xv;
1964, University of Wisconsin, no. 19; 1971, Southern
Vermont Artists, no. 5, repro.

Bibliography: Baur, Brooklyn Museum, pp. 28 & 31;
Robinson, Kennedy Galleries, p. 13

Owner: Canajoharie Library and Art Gallery,
Canajoharie, New York

In the summer of 1890, Robinson was at work
on two paintings, *At the Fountain* and *The
Watering Pots,* which are among his most successful in that they merge figurative representation and the impressionist involvement with
light and atmosphere. In both canvases, the forms
of the cistern, watering pots and the figure with
her direct gaze are firmly drawn within the
vibrant, mottled background.

The origins of the paintings lie in a group
of photographs which the artist took at Giverny
of the peasant woman, Josephine Trognon.
Whether or not the canvases were based on
photographic studies more closely related in
pose than these which survive (figs. a & b) is unknown. The relationship between the studies
and the finished works, however, is clearly dis-
cernible in the strong foreground shadows, the
sun-dappled foliage, and the sensitive shading
of the figure.

There is a smaller version of *At the Fountain*
(Baur, no. 10) which was also painted during
the summer of 1890.

31

CAPRI AND MOUNT SOLARO 1890

Oil on canvas; 18 x 22¼ inches
Signed lower right: *Th Robinson*

Provenance: George B. Wheeler, New York

Bibliography: Baur, Brooklyn Museum, pp. 31 & 60;
Robinson, Kennedy Galleries, p. 13

Owner: Museum of Fine Arts,
St. Petersburg, Florida
Gift, Friends of Art

Late in 1890, Robinson began a stay of several months in Italy, with a visit to Capri where he painted this canvas. As in so many of his Seine Valley views, his vantage point is from a hill, looking across a broad expanse, here to Mount Solaro in the distance. The sunstruck Italian architecture with its characteristic arches lies close to the slope of the hill, at times almost enveloped by the loosely-brushed foliage.

Robinson did two other paintings while at Capri, one with approximately the same dimensions as this (Baur, no. 36) and the other slightly larger (Baur, no. 38). There is reference to a third painting, *Olive Grove Capri* (Baur, no. 168) in the Theodore Robinson Estate Sale (no. 31) of 24 March 1898.

32

CHURCH IN SNOW ca. 1891

Oil on canvas; 16⅞ x 21 inches
Signed lower right: *TH. ROBINSON*

Provenance: Mrs. Agnes McCahill, ca. 1912; Miss
Frances Del Mar, New York; Mrs. Paul Blackwelder,
St. Louis; Florence Lewison Gallery, New York

Exhibitions: 1946, Brooklyn Museum, no. 40; 1962,
Florence Lewison Gallery, no. 8, repro.; 1971, Southern
Vermont Artists, no. 11

Bibliography: Robinson, Kennedy Galleries, p. 13

Owner: Mr. and Mrs. Maurice Glickman, New York

Although Robinson's pictures of winter scenes
are not numerous, the representation of snow
on the landscape with its play of reflected color
would be of obvious interest to him. Here, however, he has intentionally subordinated it in
order to emphasize the tonalities in the wall
surrounding the church yard. This flat surface
dominates the canvas with its myriad of soft
pastel hues.

The Italianate architecture of *Church in Snow*
indicates that the painting was probably done
in the early months of 1891 during the artist's
stay at Frascati, near Rome.

Fig. a
Photograph for *Two in a Boat*
3¾ x 5 inches
Courtesy of Ira Spanierman, Inc., New York

33

TWO IN A BOAT 1891

Oil on canvas board; 9¾ x 14 inches
Signed and dated lower right: *Th. Robinson—1891*

Provenance: Macbeth Gallery, New York, 1913

Exhibitions: 1895, Society of American Artists, no. 262; 1895, Macbeth Gallery, no. 26; 1895-96, Pennsylvania Academy, no. 284; 1913, Association of American Painters and Sculptors, no. 731; 1946, Brooklyn Museum, no. 229, pl. xxii

Bibliography: Baur, *Gazette des Beaux-Arts*, pp. 326-27, repro. p. 327; *Phillips Collection Catalogue*, p. 86; *Robinson*, Kennedy Galleries, p. 13; Scharf, p. 126; Coke, pp. 86-87, repro. p. 86

Owner: The Phillips Collection, Washington, D. C.

Two in a Boat demonstrates, in its compositional similarities and faint scoring, a strong dependency on the photographic study (fig. a). Elements of the photograph have been carefully transferred to the painting, the only difference being the elimination of an empty boat on the left. The colors, narrow in range and thinly brushed over the pink-primed surface of the canvas, help to create an atmosphere not unlike the slightly hazy, soft quality of the photograph.

A watercolor of the same subject executed the following year is also scored. It is slightly larger than the oil and very delicately painted. In this version, Robinson has lightened certain tonalities and produced a uniformity of values which removes all jarring notes from the gentle, tranquil scene.

34

TWO GIRLS READING IN BOAT 1892

Watercolor; 12 x 18¼ inches
Signed and dated lower right: *Th. Robinson 1892*

Owner: Private Collection, Boston

35

AFTERNOON SHADOWS 1891

Oil on canvas; 18½ x 22 inches
Signed and dated lower left: *Th. Robinson / 1891*

Provenance: Silas S. Dustin; William T. Evans; Evans Sale, American Art Assoc., New York, 31 March 1913, no. 110; Mrs. Gustav Radeke, 1920

Bibliography: Baur, Brooklyn Museum, pp. 31, 40 & 57; *Robinson*, Kennedy Galleries, p. 13

Owner: Museum of Art, Rhode Island School of Design, Providence,
Gift of Mrs. Gustav Radeke

Robinson's stay at Frascati near Rome in the first few months of 1891 was not especially productive and he was back at Giverny in April. During the following spring and summer, seemingly revitalized by the familiar landscape, he produced a group of vibrant impressionistic canvases which, in contrast to his earlier figurative works, carry further his explorations of the purely visual problems of color and of the continual shift of light. Here, the moving shadows envelope the hay field as evening approaches.

Robinson had the painting in his studio in New York two years later and noted in his Diary a comment from a visitor:

. . . he likes the 'Afternoon Shadows' but few of his friends do — think it lacks something that would make it an organic whole. He says in a field like that, however one might be struck by the beauty of the shadows, one would yet see some sky and the cutting it off so near the horizon is a bit arbitrary and artificial. (8 December 1893)

The artist, agreeing with the visitor's observation, went on to add his own comment:

Only this summer, I caught myself beginning several times a landscape with my high horizon, with absolutely no reason therefore — a reminiscence of an old fad, dating back to '79 or '80.

There is another version of this painting identical in size, but with different patterns of sunlight and shadow, thus indicating Robinson's involvement with recording the same scene at different times and under varying atmospheric conditions.

36

THE LITTLE BRIDGE (BY THE BROOK) ca. 1891

Oil on canvas; 18¼ x 23 inches
Signed lower right: *TH Robinson*

Provenance: A.P. Yorston, from the artist, 1896;
William T. Evans, 1915

Exhibitions: 1892, Williams and Everett Gallery, no.
20; 1946, Brooklyn Museum, no. 133, pl. xviii; 1962,
Florence Lewison Gallery, New York, no. 4

Bibliography: Baur, Brooklyn Museum, pp. 31 & 90;
Robinson, Kennedy Galleries, p. 13; Truettner, p. 77

Owner: Montclair Art Museum, New Jersey
Gift of William T. Evans, 1915

While at Giverny during the Summer of 1891,
Robinson quite probably painted this canvas of
his model, Josephine, standing near a little bridge.
Although he indicated in his Diary that he con-
sidered the "little bridge" a modest work, he felt,
due to its attempt at reality, that "it would wear
better than more brilliant ones done too easily
and cleverly" (23 January 1893, New York). Thus,
it would seem that for Robinson impressionism
meant primarily to record his visual experience
rather than to adhere merely to a stylistic for-
mula or a technique.

There is another version of *The Little Bridge*
(Baur, no. 132) with the same dimensions which
is signed and dated *Th. Robinson / 1891.*

37

WILLOWS (EN PICARDIE) ca. 1891

Oil on canvas; 18⅛ x 21⅞ inches
Unsigned

Provenance: Robinson Estate Sale, American Art
Assoc., New York, 24 March 1898, no. 17; George
D. Pratt, 1914

Exhibitions: 1932, Brooklyn Museum, no. 94; 1943,
Macbeth Gallery, no. 18; 1946, Brooklyn Museum,
no. 259; 1962, Florence Lewison Gallery, no. 7

Bibliography: Robinson, Kennedy Galleries, p. 13;
Hoopes, pp. 54-55, repro. p. 55

Owner: The Brooklyn Museum, New York

En Picardie, the alternative title for this canvas,
suggests that Robinson may have worked briefly
in this northern region of France, although there
is no other evidence to substantiate this possibility. Brilliant and high-keyed, the painting is
characteristic of his most purely impressionistic
works of the period 1891-92.

38

IN THE ORCHARD ca. 1891

Oil on canvas; 20 x 16¼ inches
Signed lower left: *Th. Robinson*

Provenance: Hugo Reisinger; Reisinger Sale, American Art Assoc., New York, 18 January 1916, no. 9, repro.; D. Charles

Exhibitions: 1946, Brooklyn Museum, no. 110; 1966, Kennedy Galleries, no. 38, repro.; 1971, Southern Vermont Artists, no. 4

Bibliography: Mather, p. 13, repro.; *Robinson,* Kennedy Galleries, p. 13

Owner: The Art Museum, Princeton University, New Jersey

A work of extraordinary charm, this painting is similar to another entitled *Blossoms, Giverny* (Baur, no. 20), both of which are tentatively dated 1891. One of the two versions is undoubtedly the canvas which appeared in the 1895 exhibition at the Macbeth Gallery in New York (no. 33) with the title *From a Chamber Window.* A reviewer of that exhibition aptly described the painting as "a fleeting impression of full fruit boughs, floods of sunshine and two figures, a child and a girl in light garments." (Baur, p. 66).

A painting by Robinson entitled *In the Orchard* was exhibited in the Armory Show in 1913 (no. 730) lent by William Macbeth. It was either this canvas, or one of the three others which bear the same title (see Baur, nos. 109, 111 & 112).

39

THE WATERING PLACE (HORSE DRINKING) 1891

Oil on canvas; 22 x 18 inches
Signed and dated lower right: *Th. Robinson / 1891*

Provenance: Theodore Robinson Sale, American Art Assoc., New York, 24 March 1898, no. 84; Moses H. Cone for Etta Cone, Baltimore

Exhibitions: 1892, Williams and Everett Gallery, no. 19; 1895, Macbeth Gallery, no. 23; 1895, Cotton States and International Exposition, no. 504; 1896, St. Louis Museum, no. 8; 1896, Fort Wayne Art School, no. 44; 1897, Cincinnati Museum Assoc., no. 6; 1946, Brooklyn Museum, no. 253; 1959, American Academy and National Institute of Arts and Letters

Bibliography: Cone Collection, 1934, p. 26; *The Cone Collection,* 1967, p. 68; *Robinson,* Kennedy Galleries, p. 13; Pollack, p. 34

Owner: The Baltimore Museum of Art, Cone Collection

Robinson, during the Summer and Fall of 1891 in Giverny, executed this painting of a man, whom he later identifies in his Diary as Père Trognon, watering his horse. The colors are fragile yet vibrant; the crisp greens of the foliage are in contrast to the muted pinks of the road and the building in the background. The blues and pinks reflected in the glass-like water gently blend into soft mauves.

The site of the little arched bridge with the iron railing reappears in a painting of the following year entitled *La Debacle* (cat. no. 40).

40

LA DÉBÂCLE (MARIE AT LITTLE BRIDGE) 1892

Oil on canvas; 18 x 22 inches
Signed and dated lower right: *TH Robinson / 1892*

Provenance: John Gellatly, New York, from the artist;
Vanderbilt-Barton Collection; General and Mrs.
Edward Clinton Young

Exhibitions: 1893, Society of American Artists, no.
46; 1913, Association of American Painters and
Sculptors, no. 729; 1942, California Palace of the
Legion of Honor; 1943, Denver Art Museum; 1946,
Brooklyn Museum, no. 54, pl. xxvii

Bibliography: Baur, Brooklyn Museum, pp. 25 & 28;
Robinson, Kennedy Galleries, p. 14

Owner: Scripps College, Claremont, California

In this canvas, painted early in the summer of
1892 at Giverny, the model whom Robinson
identifies in his Diary as Marie glances up from
her book. The title of the painting derives from
the volume she holds, undoubtedly Emile Zola's
La Débâcle, first published in 1892, which
Robinson read during the summer months.

Robinson records in his Diary at Giverny on 15
August 1892 that Monet, who had come to look
at some of his works, had found the painting
"amusing." On 21 December 1892, he again
mentions the canvas in a Diary entry, this time
recording its sale to the collector, John Gellatly
for $400.

41

WEDDING MARCH   1892

Oil on canvas; 19 x 24 inches
Signed lower right: *Th. Robinson*

Provenance: George B. Wheeler, New York

Exhibitions: 1970, Metropolitan Museum, no. 187, repro.; 1972, Whitney Museum, no. 61

Bibliography: Baur, Brooklyn Museum, pp. 33 & 80; Robinson, Kennedy Galleries, p. 14

Owner: Mrs. John Barry Ryan, New York

(To be exhibited in Baltimore only)

Robinson's Diary entries for July 1892 in Giverny record almost daily fluctuations in his spirit. He seemed, at times, enormously depressed about the future in general and, more specifically, about the direction in which his artistic efforts were proceeding. He does, however, on 20 July 1892, relate with considerable delight the wedding of his American friend and fellow artist Theodore Butler and Suzanne Hoschedé, one of Monet's four stepdaughters:

A great day—the marriage of Butler and Mlle. Suzanne.... The wedding party in full dress—ceremony first at the Mairie—then at the church. Monet entering first with Suzanne. Then Butler and Mme. Hoschedé—considerable feeling on the part of the parents—a breakfast at the atelier lasting most of the afternoon.

It was not until several weeks later, however, that Robinson began this canvas recording the wedding party striding briskly through the streets of Giverny. In all probability, he recalled the scene from memory, noting in his Diary on 5 August 1892:

. . . commenced my "Wedding March" my model being the groom's silk hat, lent to me by Gaston.

The leaves of the foliage sparkle in the bright light. The shadows are obvious and strong, the atmosphere, sun-filled. In its spirited brushstroke, sense of spontaneity, and well-ordered composition, the *Wedding March* is one of Robinson's most successful canvases.

42

VALLEY OF THE SEINE 1892

Oil on canvas; 25 x 32½ inches
Signed and dated lower right: *TH ROBINSON / 1892*

Provenance: George A. Hearn, New York, from the artist, 1893; Hearn Sale, American Art Assoc., New York, 25 February 1918, no. 116, repro.; Samuel T. Shaw; Shaw Sale, American Art Assoc., New York, 21 January 1926, no. 183, repro.; Macbeth Gallery, New York; W. Winter Drew; Mrs. W. Winter Drew, 1934

Exhibitions: 1893, Society of American Artists, no. 159; 1938 & 1941, Century Assoc.; 1941, Fogg Art Museum, no. 12; 1946, Brooklyn Museum, no. 240, pl. xxviii; 1964, University of Wisconsin, no. 26; 1971, Southern Vermont Artists, no. 6

Bibliography: Catalogue, Hearn Collection, no. 215 repro.; Clark, repro. p. 289; *Bulletin,* Addison Gallery, p. 19; *Handbook,* Addison Gallery, p. 51, repro.; Baur, Brooklyn Museum, p. 34; *Robinson,* Kennedy Galleries, p. 13

Owner: Addison Gallery of American Art, Phillips Academy, Andover, Massachusetts

In the summer of 1892, Robinson commenced a series of panoramic landscapes of the Seine Valley (cat. nos. 42-44), showing the village of Vernon across the river in the distance. This appears to have been a period of closeness between the American artist and Monet, the two seeing each other daily, discussing approaches to painting and commenting on one another's canvases. In this series, Robinson seemed intent on capturing the specific effects of light and shadow on the expansive view, outlining his intention in his Diary:

Commenced a Vue de Vernon most charming in morning sunlight. I will try two canvases, one, the later, will try by cloud shadows to have the river light against its banks—foreground and parts of meadow beyond in shadow. Cathedral and parts of bridge are in bright sunlight—like the old landscapes at Versailles. (4 June 1892, Giverny).

His Diary entry for the following day indicates that he had begun the second canvas. Entries continue to record his progress on the paintings, and it is obvious that he was employing much the same method with which Monet had approached his famous *Haystack* series of 1891.

Worked on my Vue de Vernon—It is begun with too much modified color—I must try for more purity. And not to work beyond the hour chosen for the effect—this is most important. (6 June 1892, Giverny).

On June 12, he indicates that he is working on two paintings simultaneously:

I had two canvases—worked on the first—grey for an hour, then the sun began to come thro' giving me a chance on the other.

The series was evidently near completion in mid-September and he showed the canvases to Monet:

A call from the Master who saw my things—he liked best the "Vue de Vernon"—the one I tho't nearest my ideal—he said it was the best landscape he had seen of mine—he liked the grey—the other sunlight one less. (15 September 1892, Giverny).

Although Diary entries suggest the existence of only two canvases, Robinson mentions on June 9 that he had begun another view, thus accounting for the third painting in the series:

Commenced a "Vue de Vernon" grey day beautiful and still—effect changed rather little for 2½-3 hours. Charming—but the sunlight with floating shadows I find more so. (9 June 1892, Giverny).

43

VALLEY OF THE SEINE FROM GIVERNY HEIGHTS 1892

Oil on canvas; 25⅞ x 32⅛ inches
Unsigned

Provenance: Robinson Estate Sale, American Art
Assoc., New York, 24 March 1898, no. 39; William T.
Evans; Evans Sale, American Art Assoc., New York,
31 January 1900, no. 250

Bibliography: Baur, Brooklyn Museum, pp. 34 & 79;
Robinson, Kennedy Galleries, pp. 13-14; Truettner,
p. 77

Owner: Corcoran Gallery of Art, Washington, D.C.

44

VALLEY OF THE SEINE 1892

Oil on canvas; 26 x 32 inches
Signed lower right: *Th. Robinson*

Provenance: Duncan Phillips, 1926; Macbeth Gallery,
New York, 1927; Francis M. Weld, 1945

Exhibitions: 1943, Macbeth Gallery, no. 9

Bibliography: Baur, Brooklyn Museum, pp. 34 & 79;
Robinson, Kennedy Galleries, p. 14

Owner: Randolph-Macon Woman's College,
Lynchburg, Virginia; Gift of Francis M. Weld, 1945

45

VALLEY OF THE SEINE ca. 1892

Oil on canvas; 18⅛ x 21¾ inches
Signed lower right: *Th. Robinson*

Provenance: Hamline Robinson, from the artist; Miss
Betty Prather; Mrs. Francis J. Oakes, Jr.; Mrs. Oakes
Colford, Brookline, Massachusetts; Hirschl and Adler
Galleries, New York

Exhibitions: 1932, Brooklyn Museum, no. 90

Bibliography: Baur, Brooklyn Museum, p. 78;
Robinson, Kennedy Galleries, p. 14

Owner: Mr. and Mrs. Raymond J. Horowitz,
New York

The hillside glows in the warm summer sun in
this view of the Seine Valley. Considerably freer
in treatment and more intimate than his
traditional Giverny landscapes, this painting appears to have been done in 1892,
Robinson's final summer abroad. In its fresh
color and animated brushstroke, it is one of his
most successful representations of the site.

46

The Old Mill

Oil on canvas; 18 x 21⅞ inches
Signed lower left: *Th. Robinson*

Provenance: Mrs. Robert W. Chambers, 1910

Exhibitions: 1946, Akron Art Institute, no. 25; 1956, Mount Holyoke, no. 48; 1961-62, American Federation of Arts, no. 6; 1962, Florence Lewison Gallery, no. 6; 1963, Albany Institute of History and Art

Bibliography: Burroughs, Metropolitan Museum, p. 306; Baur, Brooklyn Museum, p. 71; *Robinson, Kennedy Galleries*, p. 14

Owner: The Metropolitan Museum of Art, New York Gift of Mrs. Robert W. Chambers, 1910

Robinson painted the old mill at Giverny a number of times, undoubtedly drawn to the spot by the picturesque setting. In this version, the soft colors and the lack of shadow and contrast suggest that the artist was attempting to record the muted effects of a sunless, grey day. Although painted from approximately the same viewpoint as *Road by the Mill* (cat. no. 47), which is dated 1892, the restrained style and the less developed foliage indicate an earlier date.

47

Road by the Mill 1892

Oil on canvas; 20 x 25 inches
Signed lower left: *Th. Robinson—1892*

Provenance: Alfred T. and Eugenia I. Goshorn, 1924

Exhibitions: 1893, Society of American Artists, no. 73;
1893, Pennsylvania Academy, no. 111; 1895, Macbeth
Gallery, no. 22; 1895, Cotton States and International
Exposition, no. 503; 1896, Chicago Society of Artists,
no. 66; 1896, St. Louis Museum, no. 4; 1896, Fort
Wayne Art School, no. 31; 1897, Cincinnati Museum
Assoc., no. 4; 1946, Brooklyn Museum, no. 197, pl.
xxix; 1964, University of Wisconsin, no. 27

Bibliography: Baur, Brooklyn Museum, p. 33; *Robinson*, Kennedy Galleries, p. 14

Owner: Cincinnati Art Museum, Ohio

During the Summer of 1892, Robinson was at
work on this version of the mill at Giverny. In
his constant concern for the opinion of others
regarding his work, he showed the painting to
Decouchy, apparently a visitor to the village that
summer, whose comment he recorded in his
Diary:

*Decouchy liked the greens in my "Mill" which he
thinks often I modify too much—do not put down
with enough frankness.* (5 September 1892, Giverny).

Shortly thereafter, he noted Monet's observation
that there were "some undecided tones in the
'moulin' around the figure and values rather
equal" (15 September 1892, Giverny).

In the same entry, there is mention of a "lever
de lune" or moonrise, a nocturnal version of the
same site (Baur, no. 144) for which there is
also a study (Baur, no. 145).

48

THE LAYETTE 1892

Oil on canvas; 58⅛ x 36¼ inches
Signed lower right: *Th. Robinson*

Provenance: Robinson Estate Sale, American Art
Assoc., New York, 24 March 1898, no. 56; George A.
Hearn, New York; Hearn Sale, American Art Assoc.,
New York, 25 February 1918, no. 127, repro.

Exhibitions: 1893, World's Columbian Exposition,
no. 861; 1893-94, Pennsylvania Academy, no. 346;
1896, National Academy of Design, no. 45; 1932,
Museum of Modern Art, New York, no. 83; 1946,
Brooklyn Museum, no. 131; 1964, University of
Wisconsin, no. 23

Bibliography: Catalogue, Hearn Collection, no. 224,
repro.; *American Magazine of Art,* repro. p. 251;
Clark, repro. p. 765; Baur, Brooklyn Museum, p. 91;
Baur, *Gazette des Beaux-Arts,* pp. 324-25, repro. p.
325; *Robinson,* Kennedy Galleries, p. 14; Scharf,
p. 126; Coke, p. 87, repro. p. 87

Owner: Corcoran Gallery of Art, Washington, D.C.

(To be exhibited in Baltimore, Columbus and
Worcester only)

The result of Robinson's use of a carefully-posed
photographic study (fig. a) are most apparent in
The Layette of 1892. Here, vertical and hori-
zontal elements are in almost studied relationships to one another, and it is the figure of the
seated girl which provides the diagonal force in
the painting. The figure lacks animation, however, and there is a static, somewhat rigid quality
to the canvas, characteristics common to other
works which have their origins in photographs.

Robinson noted in his Diary on 30 October
1892, "Worked a.m. in Gill's Garden with

Yvonne on large Layette," indicating that he used
a live model in conjunction with the photograph
in some of his works.

There are two smaller versions of *The Layette*
(Baur, nos. 129 and 130), both probably dating
from the previous year. They, too, are based on
photographs, all three paintings differing
slightly in content and composition.

Fig. a
Photograph for
The Layette
9½ x 6¾ inches
Courtesy of
Ira Spanierman, Inc.,
New York

49

PORT BEN, DELAWARE AND HUDSON CANAL 1893

Oil on canvas; 30½ x 34¾ inches
Signed and dated lower right: *Th. Robinson '93*

Provenance: Society of American Artists, New York

Exhibitions: 1894, Society of American Artists,
no. 104, repro.; 1894, Art Institute of Chicago, no. 274;
1895, Cleveland Art Assoc., no. 219; 1895-96,
Pennsylvania Academy, no. 283; 1910, Königliche
Akademie der Kunste, p. 71; 1915, Panama-Pacific
International Exposition, no. 266, repro.; 1939-40, Art
Institute of Chicago, no. 135; 1946, Brooklyn
Museum, no. 183, pl. xxxi; 1964, University of

Wisconsin, no. 25; 1965, University of New Mexico,
no. 52, repro. p. 46

Bibliography: Paintings and Studies, Robinson Estate
Sale, no. A. (not for sale); Baur, Brooklyn Museum,
pp. 37 & 92; Young, pp. xxii & 234; *Robinson,*
Kennedy Galleries, pp. 7, 14 & 15

Owner: Pennsylvania Academy of the Fine Arts,
Philadelphia
Gift of the Society of American Artists, 1900

(To be exhibited in Baltimore only)

The Summer of 1893 was the first in five years
that Robinson did not spend in Giverny but in
his native country. In order to provide income,
he took a summer teaching position in Napanoch,
New York, in the Shawangunk Mountains near
the Delaware and Hudson Canal. There he
worked on a number of canvases of which this is
one of the most successful.

Diary entries through the summer months and
into autumn contain numerous references to the
painting as he sought to reconcile his French
Impressionist style with the elements of the
American landscape. Here, the landscape is
dominated by an enormous expanse of sky, a
subject which seems to have obsessed Robinson
during this time as quotations from his Diary
reveal:

*Painted a sky full of cumulus clouds—I must do more
skies—like all fleeting things, they are inspiring. . . .*
(Napanoch, 6 October 1893)

*My Port Ben, cumulus clouds seem to me quite
charming, luminous and gay. A word of Constables'
"that landscape painter who does not make his skies
a very material part of his composition neglects to
avail himself of one of his greatest aids."* (Napanoch,
28 October 1893)

Relatively satisfied as Robinson was with the
canvas, it was to become the center of con-

troversy after his death. A group of friends and fellow artists—among them, John LaFarge, J. Alden Weir, Will H. Low, and *Scribner's* Magazine art editor August Jaccaci—feeling that a work by Robinson should be represented in the collections of the Metropolitan Museum of Art—purchased the painting in the name of the Society of American Artists and presented it to that Museum. The Art Committee, after considerable delay, rejected it on the grounds that "it was very good of its kind, but that it was an example of a school it [the Metropolitan Museum] did not think it wise to encourage" (New York *Times*, 23 November 1900)

The landscape was subsequently presented in 1900 by the Society to the Pennsylvania Academy of the Fine Arts where Robinson had taught briefly in 1895.

50

PORT BEN, DELAWARE AND HUDSON CANAL 1893

Oil on canvas; 18¼ x 22¼ inches
Signed and dated lower right: *Th Robinson 1893*

Provenance: George B. Wheeler, New York

Exhibitions: 1965, University of New Mexico Art Gallery, no. 51

Bibliography: Baur, Brooklyn Museum, p. 73; Robinson, Kennedy Galleries, p. 15

Owner: Nebraska Art Association, Lincoln Nelle Cochrane Woods Collection

A barge glides slowly down the waterway in this smaller version of the Delaware and Hudson Canal (compare with cat. no. 49). Robinson noted some progress on this canvas

in his Diary at Napanoch on 15 September 1893:

To the white bridge—worked on grey day, but trying to keep my first impression—a very luminous sky and water—difficult as there are many kinds of greyness.

Diary entries further indicate that he was working on the two canvases simultaneously—intent, here, on capturing the subtleties of tone in the sunless landscape.

51

THE LOCK 1893

Oil on canvas; 18 x 22 inches
Signed lower right: *Th. Robinson*

Provenance: Robinson Estate Sale, American Art
Assoc., New York, 24 March 1898, no. 80; Moses H.
Cone for Etta Cone, Baltimore; Bernard M. Cone,
Greensboro, North Carolina; Harold S. Cone,
Scarsdale, New York

Exhibitions: 1895, Cotton States and International
Exposition, no. 511; 1896, St. Louis Museum, no. 25;
1897, Cincinnati Museum Assoc., no. 21

Bibliography: Baur, Brooklyn Museum, p. 68;
Robinson, Kennedy Galleries, p. 14

Owner: Claribel Cone II, Scarsdale, New York

52

CANAL SCENE 1893

Oil on canvas; 16 x 22 inches
Signed lower right: *Th. Robinson*

Provenance: Hamline Robinson, from the artist;
Mrs. C. F. Terhune, Kansas City, Missouri

Exhibitions: 1965, Great Neck Public Schools, no. 24

Bibliography: Baur, Brooklyn Museum, p. 59

Owner: Mr. and Mrs. Samuel Porter, Great Neck,
New York

The canal near Napanoch and the activity it
generated were a continual source of interest to
Robinson during the Summer and Autumn of
1893. Numerous canvases—some landscapes,

others essentially genre views—record life along the waterway. Once again, his Diary serves to reveal the manner in which he worked. Frequently, mornings with their clear sunlight were spent painting and occasionally photographing sites along the canal, while the afternoons were reserved for working on his "orchard things" in the surrounding countryside.

In these two canvases, Robinson has depicted two views of the lock—one version with the water gushing in, the other, with the lock filled. The patterns of the shadows in both indicate that they were painted at approximately the same time of the day.

53

EVENING AT THE LOCK 1893

Oil on canvas; 21¾ x 32 inches
Signed and dated lower right: *Th Robinson 1893*

Exhibitions: 1894, Society of American Artists, no. 238; 1894-95, Pennsylvania Academy, no. 263; 1895, Cotton States and International Exposition, no. 501
Bibliography: Baur, Brooklyn Museum, pp. 61-62 & 92; *Robinson,* Kennedy Galleries, p. 14
Owner: Piedmont Driving Club, Atlanta, Georgia

During the month of August at Napanoch, Robinson seemed particularly involved with this painting, intent on capturing the soft, subtle effects of dusk on the canal.

My "evening" interests me—each night two or three boats tie up and smoke from their stoves rises—the reflections are lovely in the still water, and the sky and its reflections not very gorgeous, but tender in color. (Napanoch, 15 August 1893)

Perhaps it was the stimulus of teaching which resulted in an appraisal of his approach to landscape painting:

. . . I realize more and more, the importance of the 'ensemble,' the whole thing going together, thinking quickly, grasping the whole, and working from one part to another, sky to reflection of sky, distance, foreground, etc. (Napanoch, 13 August 1893).

His application of this approach is strikingly apparent in this coherent, unified evening view of the canal.

54

THE E.M.J. BETTY 1894

Oil on canvas; 12¼ x 20 inches
Signed and dated lower right: *Th. Robinson/'94*

Provenance: Robinson Estate Sale, American Art Association, New York, 24 March 1898, no. 73; G. Schirmer; Kennedy Galleries, New York

Exhibitions: 1895, Macbeth Gallery, no. 12; 1895, Cotton States and International Exposition, no. 520; 1896, St. Louis Museum, no. 15; 1897, Cincinnati Museum Assoc., no. 13

Bibliography: Baur, Brooklyn Museum, p. 61; Robinson, Kennedy Galleries, p. 15

Owner: Private Collection, New York

With the exception of a six-week period spent teaching at Evelyn College in Princeton, New Jersey, Robinson passed the summer from 6 June to 3 September 1894 at Cos Cob, Connecticut. Delighted to be temporarily free of the oppressive city life, he wandered along the wharves and through the boat yards of this coastal town in search of subjects.

In *The E.M.J. Betty* one senses an attempt to treat the subject in an unconventional manner. The hull of the schooner is seen from beneath and at an angle. It appears to dwarf the figure and the dinghy on the left, and there are ambiguities in the spacial relationships which make it difficult to judge depth and size. It is the far shore and the bridge in the background which ultimately define the space.

55

BOATS AT A LANDING 1894

Oil on canvas; 18 x 22 inches
Unsigned

Provenance: Macbeth Gallery, New York, 1912; Alex
Morten; Mrs. Alex Morten, 1917; Macbeth Gallery,
New York, 1917; C. L. Baldwin; Baldwin *et al* Sale,
American Art Assoc., New York, 22 April 1926; Milch
Gallery, New York; Hersey Egginton, New York

Exhibitions: 1918, Union League Club, no. 35; 1923,
Macbeth Gallery, no. 9; 1946, Brooklyn Museum,
no. 22, pl. xxxiii

Bibliography: Baur, Brooklyn Museum, p. 41;
Robinson, Kennedy Galleries, p. 15

Owner: Mr. and Mrs. Meyer Potamkin

(To be exhibited in Baltimore only)

During the Summer of 1894 at Cos Cob Robinson
produced several remarkably beautiful canvases
which indicate his contentment with the site.
He had never spent an extended period of time
at the shore, and it is obvious that he was
inspired by the qualities of the intense light
reflecting off the water and its effect on the
surrounding landscape.

Diary entries frequently mention atmospheric
conditions at particular times of the day, carefully noting changes:

*Worked this a.m. three hours—a schooner unloading
coal—made a rather coarse study [see Baur, no. 41].
P.M. from the R.R. Bridge—little yachts at anchor—
a lovely hazy day—sun peeping through at 3 or 4
(12 June 1894).*

56

UNION SQUARE, NEW YORK 1895

Oil on canvas; 20 x 17 inches
Signed lower right: *Th Robinson*

Provenance: Robinson Estate Sale, American Art
Assoc., New York, 24 March 1898, no. 88;
C. Armstrong; J. F. Kosman, 1937; Macbeth Gallery,
New York

Exhibitions: 1895, National Academy of Design,
no. 153; 1895, Cotton States and International
Exposition, no. 499; 1896, St. Louis Museum, no. 1;
1896, Fort Wayne Art School, no. 28; 1897, Cincinnati
Museum Assoc., no. 1; 1938, Whitney Museum,
no. 64; 1938, Springfield Museum, no. 56; 1941, Santa
Barbara Museum, no. 99; 1943, Macbeth Gallery, no. 6;
1946, Brooklyn Museum, no. 231, pl. xxxv; 1968,
Bernard Danenberg Galleries, no. 52; 1971, Southern
Vermont Artists, no. 2, repro.

Bibliography: Robinson, Kennedy Galleries, p. 15

Owner: New Britain Museum of American Art,
New Britain, Connecticut

(To be exhibited in Baltimore, Columbus and
Worcester only)

Remarkable for the impression it conveys of a
hushed, snow-filled atmosphere is this view of
Union Square in New York City. The statue of
Washington which rises from its massive base is
silhouetted against the wintry sky and
overpowers all other elements. Diary entries
reveal that Robinson was at work on this
painting in February of 1895, and, in March of
that year, it was exhibited at the National
Academy of Design, New York, as he relates in
his Diary on 2 March 1895: "To the Academy . . .
my Wash. Monument, snow, isn't altogether
bad—the snow-flakes are, some of them,
impossibly long."

This painting is the second in a series of three
winter scenes which he did of Union Square. The
first was probably begun in January of 1894 and
not finished until sometime late in 1895 or early
in 1896. He indicates in his Diary on 12
December 1895 that he had started a third oil
which was also finished in the Winter
months of 1896.

57

FIFTH AVENUE AT TWENTY-THIRD STREET 1895

Oil on canvas; 24⅛ x 19⅛ inches
Signed lower left: *Th. Robinson*

Provenance: Charles Scribner's Sons, New York, from the artist; Robert Hosea; Fletcher, Hosea *et al* Sale, American Art Assoc., New York, 7 February 1918, no. l8; Ferdinand Howald

Exhibitions: 1946, Brooklyn Museum, no. 66; 1964, University of Wisconsin, no. 20

Bibliography: Watson, p. 84, repro. p. 64; Bolander, pp. 7 & 12; Baur, Brooklyn Museum, p. 44; *Robinson,* Kennedy Galleries, p. 15

Owner: The Columbus Gallery of Fine Arts, Ohio Ferdinand Howald Collection

The bustle of city life has been meticulously recorded in this view of Fifth Avenue near Union Square.

Commissioned by August Jaccaci, art editor of *Scribner's* Magazine and a good friend, to do a view of Fifth Avenue for publication, Robinson worked on this canvas during the Winter of 1894-95. Based on photographs supplied to him which were taken in the Fall, the painting meticulously records the varied pace of life in the city. Yet there is a rigid, almost frozen, quality to the work and a certain superficial slickness which reflects its ultimate use as an illustration. Robinson finished the canvas early in May 1895 and presented it to Jaccaci at *Scribner's* who was less than enthusiastic. Even though necessitated by financial need, Robinson acknowledged his own shortcomings at this kind of undertaking and wrote in his Diary on 9 May 1895:

I got away determined to avoid illustration—and paint, or at any rate, do my own games and not try to get commissions for work that other men will do much better. I will try some drawings . . . for possible use but for my own pleasure first.

58

LANDSCAPE 1893-95

Oil on canvas; 18 x 22 inches
Signed lower left: *Th. Robinson*

Provenance: Harry Shaw Newman Gallery, New York
Exhibitions: 1946, Brooklyn Museum, no. 125, pl. xxvi
Owner: Babcock Galleries, New York

Tree forms, the suggestion of a sloping riverbank and still water on the right are all elements of nature barely decipherable in this extraordinary canvas. The disintegration of recognizable forms, ambiguous spacial relationships, and a freedom in the use of medium all imply the search for new methods of expression which consumed Robinson upon his return to America. In this painting, impressionism has all but evolved into abstraction.

59

HAVERSTRAW ON THE HUDSON 1895

Oil on canvas; 19 x 24½ inches
Unsigned

Provenance: Kennedy Galleries, New York

Bibliography: Baur, Brooklyn Museum, p. 91;
Robinson, Kennedy Galleries, p. 15

Owner: Private Collection, New York

Robinson made the following entry in his Diary
on 5 May 1895 in New York:

*To Haverstraw again—prudently took another canvas
and it was well I did. The sun came out thro' the fog
and the morning was most lovely—parts of boats—
the tops of masts appearing thro' the fog. . . . The train
coming along—with its trail of smoke, a good detail.*

In this painting which is one of a series of three,
it is difficult to distinguish the town of
Haverstraw from the random patterning with
which the artist has depicted the Hudson River
landscape. The architecture has become patches
of greyed tones, the trees dabs of green, and the
train skirting the hillside is barely visible under
the white smoke from its engine. Although still
impressionistic, this canvas once again displays a tendency towards abstraction through
the reduction of real forms to their essential
elements.

60

A Townshend Church 1895

Oil on canvas; 13½ x 16 inches
Unsigned

Provenance: Alice Cheney, Townshend, Vermont,
from the artist

Owner: Private Collection, Boston

The summer months of 1895 which Robinson
spent at Townshend, Vermont, were not
especially fruitful. His paintings appear
unresolved, and, in his Diary, there are frequent
notations indicating his frustrations as he
sought to interpret the New England landscape,
with its totally different atmosphere, in terms
of his French experiences. During the summer,
he worked on four panoramic landscapes of the
West River Valley (see Baur, no. 256),
disheartening attempts to record the expansive
view as he had done in the *Valley of the Seine*
series at Giverny.

Somewhat more successful are the paintings
which are less grandiose in concept. In this view
of a church at Townshend, he has captured the
intimacy of a small American town.

61

ALICE CHENEY 1895

Oil on canvas; 24 x 19 inches
Unsigned

Provenance: Alice Cheney, Townshend, Vermont,
from the artist
Bibliography: Baur, Brooklyn Museum, p. 90
Owner: Private Collection, Boston

Alice was the daughter of Robinson's cousin
Agnes Cheney in whose home at Townshend,
Vermont, he lived during the Summer and
Autumn of 1895.

On 29 June he noted in his Diary:

*I took two photos of Alice, one sitting and one
standing — she has a sweet childish face — very
winning, and makes friends everywhere, and a
charming laugh and smile, but before the camera,
this changes — she is a bit conscious.*

His entry for 4 July indicates that he had begun
two canvases of Alice based on the photographs,
carefully noting the hour of the day at which he
commenced painting. He was still at work on
this version on 2 September, but to him, it was
unsuccessful:

*Worked p.m. a little with Alice — book in hand — a
banal sort of thing I must avoid as much as possible
in the future.*

Compared to his earlier figurative works, this
painting is freer and less restrained. All vestiges
of the earlier decorative style with its formality
of pose and sentimental overtones have
vanished. This thinly-brushed, fresh canvas
presents a convincing image of a light-filled
landscape on a warm, summer day.

62

SELF-PORTRAIT AT EASEL ca. 1894-95

Oil on canvas; 14 x 10 inches
Unsigned

Provenance: Kennedy Galleries, New York
Exhibitions: 1966, Kennedy Galleries, no. 14, repro.
Owner: Private Collection, New York

In a poignant self-representation, the artist sits in his studio at work on a canvas. The colors are soft, but brilliant and clear.

The painting displays a remarkably complex, almost crowded, composition which is often evident in many of Robinson's works of the period 1894-95. Objects such as the wagon wheel, the plaster cast on the floor, the chest with its open drawer, and the portfolios, their contents spilling into view, are props painstakingly arranged and locked into a rigid design.

II. Sketches

63

Boy with Raised Arm

Charcoal on paper; 14¼ x 17½ inches
Unsigned

Provenance: Hamline Robinson, from the artist;
Mrs. C. F. Terhune, Kansas City, Missouri
Exhibitions: 1966, Kennedy Galleries, repro. cover &
title page
Bibliography: Baur, Brooklyn Museum, p. 87
Owner: Private Collection, New York

On 30 March 1894 at New York, Robinson
wrote in his Diary:

*. . . Bought a watercolor by Winslow Homer. . . .
It has the same charm his work and especially
his watercolors and drawings have always had
for me. . . .* [The name erased] *was surprised at
my wanting it—as I paint so different.*

As the entry indicates, Robinson was a life-long
admirer of Homer, and this charcoal drawing of
a young boy seems reminiscent of elements in
Homer's art.

One feels often in Robinson's art a sense of
reworking and refining as he labored to carry
each work to an often unobtainable ideal. Yet
here, with a paucity of line and an extraordinarily
delicate touch but with great assurance, he has
rendered the boy, one arm raised, mouth slightly
open, his eyes fixed in a distant gaze. Though
essentially flat, there is the suggestion of form in
the placement of the hand on the waist and in
the subtle shading under the hat, on the face and
neck, and in the folds of the smock. This fresh,
sensitive charcoal study stands as one of Robinson's most eloquent statements.
eloquent statements.

64

SKETCHBOOK 1871-ca.1876

Pencil and wash on paper
Page size: 3⅞ x 6⅛ inches
95 leaves; 67 drawings

Provenance: Hamline Robinson, from the artist;
Mrs. C. F. Terhune, Kansas City, Missouri

Owner: Ira Spanierman, Inc., New York

The drawings contained in this sketchbook are
among Robinson's earliest known works, dating
from the years 1871 through ca.1876, a period
which saw him move from boyhood in Evansville,
Wisconsin, to student life in Paris. The drawings
are predominately figurative, depicting people in
various informal poses—many are merely
outlines suggesting form; others are detailed
and beautifully finished. There are also a small
number of renderings done after canvases by
Chardin and Carolus-Duran.

Worthy of special mention is a group of drawings
done in the Central Park Zoo during the Autumn
months of 1874, shortly after Robinson's arrival
in New York. Although modest, they are
extremely appealing in their sensitivity to the
characteristics of the animals depicted.

Nov. 21.
'74

Mrs Baker
May 5. '75

68

The Belvidere
Oct 31. 74

Central Park,
Oct. 31. 74.

64

64

65

SKETCHBOOK 1876-77

Pencil on paper
Page size: 8½ x 11½ inches
30 leaves extant: 30 drawings

Inscribed on reverse of front cover: *Theo. Robinson—
1876 / 81 Blv. Mt. Parnasse / Paris*

Provenance: Hamline Robinson, from the artist;
Mrs. C. F. Terhune, Kansas City, Missouri
Owner: Ira Spanierman, Inc., New York

The contents of this sketchbook record a wide
range of geographical locales which serve to plot
Robinson's route from Le Havre through
Normandy to Paris on his first journey abroad in
1876. Drawings of buildings and architectural
views at Rouen, Jumièges, Caen, Bayeux and
Paris are interspersed with genre scenes, portraits,
and sketches after works by Puvis de Chavannes,
Germain Pilon and others. Most of the drawings
are inscribed indicating their source.

Many of the architectural drawings, especially
those done at Rouen, are highly detailed
renderings, and in their contrasts of light and
dark areas, they are not unlike Robinson's
paintings of the same period (see cat. no. 1).
Other architectural sketches are delicate and
essentially flat, merely delineating the
boundaries of forms. In some of these, Robinson
has made notations on the drawings as to color
value and the nature of the building materials.

Perhaps among the most successful drawings in
the sketchbook are the portraits, many of which
are carefully-drawn sensitive character studies,
testifying to his initial preoccupation as a youth
with portraiture.

Porte d'une ancienne chapelle
St Romain

2½ p.m.

66

17 Sept. 44
Gray morning

14 Sept '94

66

SKETCHBOOK 1894

Pencil on paper
Page size: 4 x 6½ inches

33 leaves; 27 drawings

Inscribed on reverse of front cover: *Theo. Robinson / Cos Cob. June '94.*

Provenance: Hamline Robinson, from the artist; Mrs. C. F. Terhune, Kansas City, Missouri

Owner: Ira Spanierman, Inc., New York

The sketches in this little book with their occasional notations record Robinson's activities from June to December of 1894. During this period, he was primarily at Cos Cob, Connecticut; Princeton and Brielle, New Jersey. The last few leaves dated December 1894 contain subjects around New York.

Of special interest are the Cos Cob scenes of placid coves on the coast, many with sailboats, their vertical masts in contrast to the flat horizon. These appear to be essentially quick sketches, minimal in their representation of detail. More important to Robinson seemed to be the varied effects of light on water and the surrounding landscape. Gentle shading as well as notation of the time of day when the sketches were done indicate his continuing involvement in atmospheric changes. Scattered throughout the sketchbook are lists of paintings, accounts, train schedules and the like. The rather amusing leaf, the text of which is quoted below, would seem to indicate one of his methods for titling a finished work:

Lawn with Pine trees.
Evelyn.
Pines of Evelyn
Evelyn Pines
Among the Pines.
Under the Pine trees.
The Pines at Evelyn
Pines at Evelyn
Groves of Academe
Grove of Academe.

Dec. 24 '94

Selected Bibliography

EXHIBITIONS

1946, Akron Art Institute, Akron, Ohio. *America Paints Outdoors.*

1963. Albany Institute of History and Art. *Theodore Robinson.*

1959, American Academy of Arts and Letters and The National Institute of Arts and Letters, New York. *The Impressionist Mood in American Painting.*

1961-62, American Federation of Arts, New York. *Monet and the Giverny Group* (circulating).

1964-66, American Federation of Arts, New York. *100 Years of American Realism: Watercolors and Posters* (circulating).

1889, American Water Color Society, New York. *Annual Exhibition.*

1894, Art Institute of Chicago, Chicago. *Annual Exhibition.*

1939-40, Art Institute of Chicago, Chicago. *Half A Century of American Art.*

1913, Association of American Painters and Sculptors, New York. *International Exhibition of Modern Art,* (at the Armory, New York).

1968, Bernard Danenberg Galleries, New York. *Our American Heritage.*

1890, Boston Art Club, Boston. *Annual Exhibition.*

1892, Boston Art Club, Boston. *Annual Exhibition.*

1932, Brooklyn Museum, New York. *Exhibition of Paintings by American Impressionists and Other Artists of the Period 1880-1900.*

1946, Brooklyn Museum, New York. *Theodore Robinson.*

1942, California Palace of the Legion of Honor, San Francisco. *75 Years of American Painting.*

1938, Century Association, New York.

1941, Century Association, New York.

1960, Charles E. Slatkin Galleries, New York. *Claude Monet and the Giverny Artists.*

1896, Chicago Society of Artists, Chicago.

1897, Cincinnati Museum Association, Cincinnati. *A Collection of Work by the Late Theodore Robinson Embracing Twenty-One Studies and Pictures.*

1895, Cleveland Art Association, Cleveland. *Annual Exhibition.*

1895, Cotton States and International Exposition, Atlanta.

1943, Denver Art Museum, Denver. *Masterpieces of American Painting.*

1962, Detroit Institute of Arts, Detroit. *American Paintings and Drawings from Michigan Collections.*

1962, Florence Lewison Gallery, New York. *Theodore Robinson*

1965, Florence Lewison Gallery, New York. *A Choice of Americans.*

1941, Fogg Art Museum, Harvard University, Cambridge, Massachusetts. *American Landscape Painting, George Inness to George Bellows.*

1896, Fort Wayne Art School, Fort Wayne, Indiana. *Central Art Association Exhibit.*

1965, Great Neck Public Schools, Great Neck, New York. *An Exhibition of 150 Years of American Painting for the Sesquicentennial Celebration of the Great Neck Public Schools.*

1961, John Herron Art Museum, Indianapolis. *Romantic America.*

1961, Institute of Arts, Flint, Michigan. *American Painting, 1860-1960.*

1963, International Business Machines, Corporation, New York. *Realism: An American Heritage.*

1886, Inter-State Industrial Exposition of Chicago, Chicago. *14th Annual Exhibition.*

1889, Inter-State Industrial Exposition of Chicago, Chicago. *17th Annual Exhibition.*

1890, Inter-State Industrial Exposition of Chicago, Chicago. *18th Annual Exhibition.*

1966, Kennedy Galleries, Inc., New York. *Theodore Robinson: American Impressionist, 1852-1896.*

1910, Königliche Akademie der Kunste, Berlin. *Ausstellung Amerikanischer Kunst.*

1940, Los Angeles County Museum of Art, Los Angeles. *The Development of Impressionism.*

1895, Macbeth Gallery, New York. *Theodore Robinson.*

1913, Macbeth Gallery, New York.

1923, Macbeth Gallery, New York. *Paintings by Emil Carlsen, Theodore Robinson, J. Alden Weir.*

1939, Macbeth Gallery, New York. *American Watercolors: Past and Present.*

1943, Macbeth Gallery, New York. *Theodore Robinson.*

1970, Metropolitan Museum of Art, New York. *19th Century America, Paintings and Sculpture.*

1956, Mount Holyoke College, Massachusetts. *French and American Impressionism.*

1932, Museum of Modern Art, New York. *American Painting and Sculpture, 1862-1932.*

1939, Museum of Modern Art Gallery, Washington, D. C. *A Century of American Painting.*

1890, National Academy of Design, New York. *Annual Exhibition.*

1895, National Academy of Design, New York. *Annual Exhibition.*

1896, National Academy of Design, New York. *Annual Exhibition.*

1935, National Academy of Design, New York. *A Selection of Paintings from the Permanent Collection.*

1931, Newark Museum, Newark. *American Painting from 1700 to 1900.*

1915, Panama-Pacific International Exposition, San Francisco.

1891, Pennsylvania Academy of the Fine Arts, Philadelphia. *Annual Exhibition.*

1893-94, Pennsylvania Academy of the Fine Arts, Philadelphia. *Annual Exhibition.*

1894-95, Pennsylvania Academy of the Fine Arts, Philadelphia. *Annual Exhibition.*

1895-96, Pennsylvania Academy of the Fine Arts, Philadelphia. *Annual Exhibition.*

1944, Phillips Memorial Gallery, Washington, D. C. *The American Paintings of the Phillips Collection.*

1915, Reading Public Museum, Pennsylvania.

1896, St. Louis Museum of Fine Arts, St. Louis. *A Collection of Twenty-Seven Pictures and Studies by the Late Theodore Robinson.*

1889, Salon, Paris.

1941, Santa Barbara Museum of Art, Santa Barbara. *Painting Today and Yesterday in the United States.*

1889, Society of American Artists, New York. *Annual Exhibition.*

1890, Society of American Artists, New York. *Annual Exhibition.*

1893, Society of American Artists, New York. *Annual Exhibition.*

1894, Society of American Artists, New York. *Annual Exhibition.*

1895, Society of American Artists, New York. *Annual Exhibition.*

1971, Southern Vermont Artists, Inc., Manchester. *Theodore Robinson, the 19th Century Vermont Impressionist.*

1938, Springfield Museum of Fine Arts, Massachusetts.

1918, Union League Club, New York. *Exhibition by American Artists from the Collection of C. Lansing Baldwin, Esq.*

1935, Union League Club, New York. *Exhibition of Paintings by American Artists Lent by The Metropolitan Museum of Art.*

1964, University of Iowa Gallery of Art. Iowa City. *Impressionism and its Roots.*

1965, University of New Mexico Art Gallery, Albuquerque. *Impressionism in America.*

1964, University of Wisconsin, Memorial Union Gallery, Madison. *Theodore Robinson.*

1938, Whitney Museum of American Art, New York. *A Century of American Landscape Painting, 1800-1900.*

1942, Whitney Museum of American Art, New York. *A History of American Watercolor Painting.*

1972, Whitney Museum of American Art, New York. *18th and 19th Century American Art From Private Collections.*

1892, Williams and Everett Gallery, Boston. *Paintings in Oil and Pastel by Theodore Robinson and Theodore Wendel.*

1958, Woman's College, University of North Carolina, Greensboro, North Carolina. *The Cone Collection.*
1893, World's Columbian Exposition, Chicago.

PUBLICATIONS

American Impressionists. New York: Hirschl and Adler Galleries, 1968.
American Magazine of Art, IX, no. 6 (April 1918): 251.
Baur, John I. H. *Theodore Robinson, 1852-1896.* New York: The Brooklyn Museum, 1946.
_____. "Photographic Studies by an Impressionist." *Gazette des Beaux-Arts,* series VI, XXX (Oct.-Dec. 1946).
Bolander. "Ferdinand Howald and His Collection." *Bulletin of the Columbus Gallery of Fine Arts* (Jan. 1931).
Brinton, Christian. "American Paintings at the Panama-Pacific Exposition." *International Studio* (Aug. 1915).
"Brooklyn Honors Memory of Theodore Robinson." *Art Digest* (15 November 1946): 9.
Bulletin of the Addison Gallery of American Art (1936).
Burroughs, Bryson. *Catalogue of Paintings.* 9th ed. New York: The Metropolitan Museum of Art, 1931.
Campbell, Pearl H. "Theodore Robinson: A Brief Historical Sketch." *Brush and Pencil,* IV (Sept. 1899): 287-89.
Catalogue. Northampton: Smith College Museum of Art, 1937.
Catalogue of the Collection of Foreign and American Paintings Owned by George A. Hearn. New York, 1908.
Catalogue Deluxe of the Department of Fine Arts for the Panama-Pacific International Exhibition. San Francisco, 1893.
Clark, Eliot. "Theodore Robinson." *Art in America* (Oct. 1918).
_____. "Theodore Robinson: A Pioneer Impressionist." *Scribner's,* XXX, no. 6 (Dec. 1921).
Coke, Van Deren. *The Painter and the Photograph.* Albuquerque: New Mexico Press, 1972.
Cone Collection of Baltimore, Maryland. Baltimore: Etta Cone, 1934.

The Cone Collection. Rev. ed. Baltimore: The Baltimore Museum of Art, 1967.
"First and Last U. S. Impressionists: Theodore Robinson and A. C. Goodwin." *Art News,* 45 (Dec. 1946): 20-21.
Garland, Hamlin. "Theodore Robinson." *Brush and Pencil* 4 (Sept. 1899): 285-86.
Handbook of Paintings . . . in the Permanent Collection. Andover, Massachusetts: Addison Gallery of American Art, 1939.
Harrison, Birge. "With Stevenson at Grez." *The Century Magazine,* 93, no. 2 (Dec. 1916).
Hoopes, Donelson F. *The American Impressionists.* New York: Watson-Guptill Publications, 1972.
Huth, Hans. "Impressionism Comes to America." *Gazette des Beaux-Arts,* XXIX (1946): 225-252.
Illustrated Sales Catalogue: William M. Bunn, et al. Sale. Philadelphia: Samuel T. Freeman and Co., 1914.
Levy, Florence N. "Theodore Robinson." *Bulletin of the Metropolitan Museum of Art* (July 1906): 111-12.
Lewison, Florence. *Theodore Robinson: America's First Impressionist.* New York: Florence Lewison Gallery, 1963.
_____. "Theodore Robinson and Claude Monet," *Apollo,* 78 (Sept. 1963): 208-11.
Low, Will H. *A Chronicle of Friendships, 1873-1900.* New York: Charles Scribner's Sons, 1908.
Mather, F. S., Jr. "American Paintings at Princeton University." *Records at the Museum of Historic Art* (Fall 1943).
Paintings and Studies by the Late Theodore Robinson. New York: American Art Assoc., 1898.
Paintings in the Art Institute of Chicago: A Catalogue of the Picture Collection. Chicago: Art Institute of Chicago, 1961.
The Phillips Collection Catalogue. Washington, D. C.: Thames and Hudson, 1952.
Phillips, Duncan. *A Collection in the Making.* New York: E. Weyhe, 1926.
Pollack, Barbara. *The Collectors: Dr. Claribel and Miss Etta Cone.* Indianapolis-New York: The Bobbs-Merrill Co., Inc., 1962.
Richardson, E. P. *A Short History of Painting in America: The Story of 450 Years.* New York, 1963.
Robinson, Theodore. "Claude Monet" in *Modern*

French Masters: A Series of Biographical and Critical Reviews by American Artists. John C. van Dyke (ed.) New York: The Century Company, 1896 [This essay was first published in *Century Magazine* (Sept. 1892): 696-701].

_____. "Jean-Baptiste-Camille Corot" in *Modern French Masters: A Series of Biographical and Critical Reviews by American Artists.* John C. van Dyke (ed.). New York: The Century Company, 1896.

Robinson, Theodore: American Impressionist, 1852-1896. New York: Kennedy Galleries, Inc., 1966.

Scharf, Aaron. *Art and Photography.* Baltimore: Allen Lane, The Penguin Press, 1969.

Seitz, William C. *Claude Monet.* New York: Harry N. Abrams, Inc., 1960.

Truettner, William H. "William T. Evans: Collection of American Paintings," *American Art Journal,* III, no. 2 (Fall 1971).

Watson, Forbes. "American Collections, No. 1 — The Ferdinand Howald Collection." *The Arts* (August 1925).

Young, Dorothy Weir. *The Life and Letters of J. Alden Weir.* New Haven: Yale University Press, 1960.

PHOTOGRAPH CREDITS

Page xix, Peter A. Juley & Son, New York; cat. nos. 1 & 3, Oliver Baker, New York; cat. nos. 2, 11, 60 & 61, Herbert P. Vose, Wellesley Hills, Massachusetts; cat. no. 4, Taylor & Dull, Inc., New York; cat. nos. 8, 10 & 32, Geoffrey Clements, New York; cat. nos. 9, 27 & 45, John D. Schiff, New York; cat. nos. 12, 18-20, 39 & 63-65, Duane Suter, Baltimore; cat. no. 17, Frick Art Reference Library, New York; cat. nos. 25 & 26, Walter Russell, New York; cat. no. 41, Milch Art Gallery, New York; cat. no. 52, Thomas Feist; cat. no. 53, Jerome Drown, Atlanta, Georgia; cat. no. 55, Biago Pinto, Philadelphia; cat. no. 56, E. Irving Blomstrann, New Britain, Connecticut; cat. no. 59, Brenwasser, New York

Designed by Gerard A. Valerio, Edita Graphics, Inc., Annapolis, Maryland
Composed in Linofilm Trump by General Typographers, Inc., Washington, D. C.
Printed on Mohawk Superfine and Strathmore Artlaid by The Art Litho Co., Baltimore, Maryland
Bound by the Graphic Arts Finishing Co., Baltimore.